STING AND
•
THE POLICE

Also Published by Ballantine Books:

STING AND THE POLICE

Ray Nikart

BALLANTINE BOOKS • NEW YORK

Library of Congress Catalog Card Number: 84-90914

ISBN 0-345-32179-0

Manufactured in the United States of America

First Edition: January 1985

Front cover photo: Bob Alfor/Star File Photos
Back cover photo: Laura Levine
Photo research: Amanda Rubin
Interior book design: Michaelis/Carpelis Design Associates, Inc.

Dedicated to the Ones I Love
M. and P. Nikart, Jill Merrill, Jan

CONTENTS

INTRODUCTION

"I hope that someone gets my . . . message in a bottle."
                                              —the Police

*A*ugust 18, 1983: It is a muggy midsummer's Thursday night in New York City, the oppressive humidity giving way to lightning flashes, the crackle of thunder, and intermittent showers. The subway car is packed with fans streaming into Shea Stadium for the year's most anticipated rock event. The inevitable comparisons to the Beatles' legendary performance eighteen years ago is on everybody's lips.

In a little over six years, Sting, Stewart Copeland, and Andy Summers have risen to the summit as members of the Police, riding high atop the U.S. charts with a number one album, *Synchronicity*, and a number one single, "Every Breath You Take." This concert will be the culmination of the gigs played in sweaty clubs performed before a handful of patrons as well as the missed opportunities represented by previous associations, old bands, and former colleagues. Through ambition, tireless hard work, talent, and more than a little luck, the Police are anointed heavyweight champs, Top of the Pops, the world's most popular rock 'n' roll band, with tonight's show.

As the faithful file into Shea, the downpour lets up long enough for the Athens, Georgia, pop rock of REM and the black leather hard rock of Joan Jett, the two opening acts, to play. But it is clear from the start whom this seventy-thousand-plus throng has come to see. The klieg lights that illuminate the stadium dim to a crescendo of cheers. Sting, Andy, and Stewart bound onstage, and the din is deafening. The giant video-screen lights up with images of the band, and the crystal clear sound system captures every nuance, turning the huge arena into an intimate living room.

The jubilant strain of the band's hits fills the stadium— from the speeded-up pseudopunk drive of "Next to You," the very first track from their debut LP, *Outlandos D'Amour*, to the melancholy plaint of "Walking in Your Footsteps" from *Synchronicity*, the trio refuses to let go of the crowd, which hangs on every syllable. A cool breeze sweeps Shea Stadium, a refreshing postscript to the summer shower.

Sting, completely in control, seems almost oblivious at center stage to his two partners, equally in worlds of their own. Blond-haired Summers strums his guitar with exaggerated heavy metal hero gestures, thick, chunky power chords cushioning drummer Stewart Copeland's feverish muscular beat. The magic is in the combination of three individual orbits soaring above the sum of their collective parts.

Suddenly the familiar strains of the band's first-ever hit, the echoed reggae intro that signals "Roxanne"— Sting's plaintive ode to an anonymous lady of the night sparked by his visit to a Parisian red-light district on an early Police tour—are heard. The klieg lights flash on and the stadium shakes from its rafters as the audience rises as one and chants along with the chorus, practically drowning out the singer, much to Sting's apparent delight: "Roxanne . . ." The group then runs through another early hit, "Can't Stand Losing You," their follow-up to "Roxanne." The evening is a complete triumph.

Flashback to five years earlier, a mid-November weeknight at CBGB's, 1978. The long narrow club on New York City's Bowery sports a bar that runs nearly the length of its limited space. Bums spill out of adjoining doorways. Neon-lit beer signs and Xeroxed posters are the only concession to decoration. The one-time biker hangout has become famous as the birthplace of punk rock or New Wave, the late seventies musical movement that came simultaneously out of New York and London, sporting groups like the Sex Pistols, the Clash, the Ramones and Blondie, Patti Smith, Television, the Jam, and Talking Heads, all espousing ideals of youth, change, and revolution.

On this particular Wednesday eve, the venerable punk shrine looks even shabbier than usual, with a tiny gathering of perhaps twenty-five stragglers staring into their beers with boredom in their eyes. Even owner Hilly Krystal's dog dozes off. The legions of scene makers, hipsters, artists, writers, and chick hangers-on who usually populate the place are nowhere to be seen. A glimpse of the future of rock 'n' roll seems hardly likely. Ambling on for their second set is an English band that has made their U.S. debut only a month before at this very site. The word of mouth on the Police is none too promising either. Apparently the lead singer/bassist used to play in a traditional jazz big band; the drummer, whose brother Miles manages the group, came from a progressive rock band named Curved Air; while the guitarist once played with Eric Burdon and the Animals. For punk purists, the combination of the band's old-fashioned background and the dark roots underneath their dyed punk-cut hair leaves the Police wide open to accusations of bandwagon jumping.

The first portion of the set does little to dispel that notion: the band rushes through the protopunk set in typical fashion; the songs speed by without registering. How have these guys managed to tour America with only an import single available, an obscure reggae novelty track called . . .

"Roxanne . . ." Suddenly Sting's sad vocals wrap around the refrain, and the group's measured, deliberate background combine to make the small crowd sit up and take notice. The song's a hit.

But "Roxanne" was only the start. What followed is an incredible success story for three musicians who came together from very different backgrounds to form one of the most successful rock 'n' roll groups of all time, with a string of five gold or platinum albums, a succession of worldwide hit singles, multiple Grammy awards, and sold-out international tours.

Their success crosses many boundaries. The Police are admired equally by teenyboppers and rock critics, denim-clad rockers and spiky punks, English and American fans, along with followers in such disparate parts of the globe as South Africa, New Zealand, Canada, Italy, Japan, Germany, Egypt, India, and Venezuela.

Although it might seem like the Police's climb to the top of the rock pile has taken place overnight, Sting, Stewart, and Andy have worked long and hard to achieve their breakthrough. In many ways their joint ambitions were fueled by years of frustration and disappointment. The mournful, contemplative edge to much of the Police's music is rooted in the individual members' pasts and belies the material's bouncy beat.

The Police story is one of resilience and persistence in

the wake of resistance, getting what you want by any means open to you, overcoming through endurance, hard work, perspiration, and inspiration. As well as the most important ingredient of all: MAGIC.

THE POLICE'S DARK ROOTS: PORTRAIT OF STING AS A YOUNG MAN

"I'll fight tooth and nail until I'm in command."
—Sting, in *Rolling Stone*, February 19, 1981

"*E*verybody in the business knows in his heart of hearts what it takes to be successful," Sting said. "Whether you've got the guts to go through with that or not is another matter. The blueprint was really fashioned by the Beatles. The Beatles made these great plans for an odyssey: this British group from Liverpool, nobody knows them, and then they conquer the world."

The Police have three members who each contribute something very important to the group, but their focal point is the enigma known as Sting, the band's bass-playing singer/songwriter. Drummer Stewart Copeland had the vision and guitarist Andy Summers the sound, but it was Sting who provided the Ace Face, the superstar quality that put the Police over the top. Alternately lovable and hateful, always keenly ambitious, Sting wrote and sang the songs that catapulted the Police to the head of their class.

He's been called ruthless, but Sting floundered for the first twenty-five years of his life before he had achieved any measurable success. He couldn't decide whether to stay in school or get a job, be a musician or a teacher, a jazzer or a rocker. His insecurities stemmed from a working-class Catholic background that discouraged rebellion and nonconformity, a childhood both awkward and un-happy.

Sting was born Gordon Matthew Sumner on October 2, 1951, in Wallsend, a blue-collar region of Newcastle in the northeast of England that had fallen on hard times with the decline of Britain's postwar industries. The borough was plagued with pollution, alcoholism, lack of housing and jobs, as well as miserable weather: windy and cold.

The city is located alongside the Tyne River. "It's an old boom town," Sting would tell *Rolling Stone* in March 1982, "that never recovered from the Thirties recession in coal mining, shipbuilding, heavy industry." The Sumners lived by a shipyard.

"They'd build tankers there. Every six months they'd build one up to be this towering great hull over the street. The pointy end would literally hang over the street; that's my first-ever memory of home."

Gordon was the eldest child of Eric and Audrey Sumner. He has a brother, Philip, and two sisters, Angela and Anita. After working at one of the local engineering factories, his father became a milkman once he was married, managing and then finally owning a small dairy. His mother was a hairdresser and a classically trained piano player who stopped working for a few years after she had Sting, when she was eighteen.

Although his parents were never poor, Sting was not a happy child. He remembers his family always on the verge of splitting up, though his parents finally divorced only a few years ago.

In a 1979 interview with *Rolling Stone*, he put down his background but four years later told an interviewer from the same magazine he was sorry he did.

"I suppose that part of my egocentric drive is an attempt to transcend my family and childhood. . . . I lived in a working class area and the whole thing for me was escape."

It was just that blend of arrogance and insecurity that turned young Gordie into a Newcastle punk, fifties style, playing football (soccer), chasing birds (girls), getting into rumbles, sneaking ales at the local pub, and hanging out at the local cinema. But Sting also loved learning. He was an avid reader and an altar boy at church, where he learned the entire service in Latin. Even as a child, Sting hovered between angel and devil, a dualism he'd maintain into adulthood.

Sting was always a good student, too, especially in English. He would write "doggerel verse, with alacrity, without thinking," he once boasted to an English journalist. His grandmother Agnes turned the inquisitive youngster on to books like *Treasure Island*, while Sting pored through the periodicals at Grandma's house, like the English humor magazine *Punch!*. He also enjoyed Superman comics.

At about the same age Sting began to take an interest in music, sitting underneath his mom's piano listening to her play. As soon as he could reach the keys, Sting taught himself. When he was eight years old, Gordon received his first guitar, left with the family for safekeeping by an uncle who moved to Canada.

Sting immediately learned the instrument and eagerly performed for any visiting relatives. But these moments of creativity were accompanied by frustration. He had few role models, and as a Catholic in a Protestant country, he often felt like an outsider. He went to a strict Jesuit school where beatings were the order of the day, cultivating his hatred of authority. One year he found himself disciplined seven times by the dean, who administered "six of the best" with a wooden cane.

"His was a chore straight out of *Tom Brown's School*

Days," Sting said. "You bent over a chair and the man flailed you with all his might. You didn't want to cry, but after three whacks you always broke down, because there was an involuntary welling up of pain and mortification. It was one of the most humiliating experiences of my life."

In addition, at nine years of age Sting had grown to practically his full five-foot-nine height, making him the butt of school yard jibes. Teasing classmates called him "Lurch," the name of the butler from the old *Munsters* series, while Sting would desperately try to make friends by hiding his superior wit and intelligence.

Sting had received a scholarship to attend the school and found himself surrounded by paying classmates from wealthy families, another jolt to his fragile ego. He grew up without many close friends, a loner.

The importance of social class was something that would never elude Sting. While he studied, the neighborhood kids he'd grown up with kicked around a soccer ball. He was lonely and he turned to his friend, the battered acoustic guitar left to him by his uncle. He practiced often, strumming along idly to Beatles and Stones records, trying to rid himself of his thick northern England accent. As a star athlete in his midteens, he ranked third in the country in the hundred-meter and two-hundred-meter sprints. He finished third in a national competition and promptly quit running, just like that. Third place just wasn't good enough.

"A working class boy in England can make it through soccer, through rock music, and, to a certain extent, through the educational system," Sting recalled. "Back in the thirties, when my father was born, his place was decided for him early on, and it stuck. . . . He's a reserved man, not a sagelike type, and the only advice he ever gave me was to leave home and join the navy, to get out of the system."

Sting took his father's advice. While at school, he tended toward the symbols of middle-class rebellion: the beatnik writing of Jack Kerouac, the English poetry of Ted Hughes, jazz albums by Charles Mingus and Thelonious Monk. Sting would listen to them for hours, forcing himself to like the discordant new sounds.

He also liked pop music, though—Bob Dylan, Motown soul, and, as most of his generation, the Beatles and Stones. But the Fab Four became the standard by which Sting would judge his own success, though he often fretted that their achievements could never be overshadowed. Sting's own high-pitched tenor evoked that of his idol, Paul McCartney.

The first band a fourteen-year-old Sting ever saw live was the Graham Bond Organization, in 1965. The band featured future Cream bassist Jack Bruce and appeared at Newcastle's leading venue, the Club A Go Go, where the Animals had recorded a live album with blues great Sonny Boy Williamson. In a twist of fate, the second band Sting went to see was Zoot Money and the Big Roll Band, with a cherubic guitarist named Andy Somers, who would later change his last name to Summers.

Sting went from guitar to bass after seeing Jack Bruce. He'd listen to his records, pick out the bass lines, and learn them. But music did not seem the most likely way for Sting to move up the social ladder and get out of Newcastle. He continued to study and, despite misgivings, took university entrance examinations.

Sting's intensity carried over into his personal life, and he's never been one to treat romance lightly. He had a pair of intense affairs, which ended unhappily. Despite the anguish caused by each, Sting has admitted to using the experiences to help him write emotional songs like "The Bed's Too Big without You" and "Every Breath You Take."

While getting ready to take his exams in 1969, Sting took a variety of odd jobs. He was a bus conductor in Newcastle, where he enjoyed performing in front of the riders, a skill he would also employ as a schoolteacher before finding his true calling as a rock star. Unsatisfactory test results led Sting to reconsider his plans to attend college, so he remembered his father's counsel, applied for a seaman's card, and signed on with Princess Cruises as a bassist in a shipboard dance band, the Ronnie Pierson Trio. He spent the summer sailing around the Mediterranean and began to realize that music could be his means of escape.

"I came upon music entirely by accident," he said, "and I developed it entirely on my own, even though my mother played piano. As far as I was concerned, music was just another barrier to shut the world out; what bothered me most as an adolescent was the sensation that I didn't know if I had any place in it. I always regarded myself as a freak, and spent a lot of time trying to fit in. The effort always ended in failure, because I *was* different. I wouldn't be where I am if I didn't have the feeling of 'apartness' that allows me to express myself in a very exhibitionist and noisy way.

"I knew I would never be a part of normal society, but if I didn't find some freedom, considering the life that likelihood seemed to have planned for me in my teens, I think that eventually madness would have interceded."

After the summer Gordon enrolled at Warwick University (despite his disappointing test results) but quit after a single term out of boredom. He ended up digging ditches, then he went to the opposite end of the work spectrum and donned a suit for a civil service job as an accountant with the Inland Revenue branch, but that lasted only six months. Not a responsible employee, he arrived late, left early, took four-hour lunches, and reread his favorite book, a well-thumbed copy of James Joyce's *Ulysses*. He was almost fired, practically impossible for anyone in a civil service job.

"I swore I'd never work in an office again," he said.

"I wanted to be a musician, but I didn't want to stick my handkerchief on a stick and just walk off."

So a still-confused Sting applied to Northern Counties Teacher Training College in Newcastle, where he was accepted for the fall 1971 term. It marked a return to his family, his roots—a prospect that must have bruised his ego no small amount. He entered a program for a Teacher's Certificate in English and Music. Despite his scorn for the academic environment, he liked teaching. He saw an area where he could influence young kids for the better; he tried to create a learning environment "opposite to the way I was taught." He also needed the security, which in turn allowed him to continue his pursuit of music.

Sting attended teacher's college for three years. After graduating and being accredited in July 1974, he "slogged" to Newcastle to teach English and coach the soccer team at a convent school.

He began hanging out at the Wheatsheaf, a Newcastle pub used by jazz musicians for informal jams. The resident rhythm section at the club was called the Phoenix Jazzmen, and Sting would occasionally fill in for the bass player, Ernie, getting blisters from his big double bass.

A fellow student at teacher's college who also filled in on bass for the Jazzmen, Gerry Richardson, turned out to be a major influence on Sting's life and career. The Leeds-born Richardson went to a local bistro on the recommendation of his girlfriend to check out a bassist named Gordon whom she'd seen doing soft-rock numbers by sensitive singer/songwriters like James Taylor. He wasn't much interested until he found out the young folkie knew a drummer with a van and a PA. Gerry hired him on the spot, forming a band with Sting called Earthrise.

Sting was a little shy about singing, though he did croon a mean version of the Ashton, Gardner, and Dyke hit "Resurrection Shuffle." Sharing a love of flashy jazz riffing, Gerry and Sting hit it off immediately. But even friendship would not curb Sting's musical ambitions. When Richardson left his post as bassist with the Jazzmen, Sting stepped in and brought along his electric bass, moving the traditional band into the modern world of rock 'n' roll.

It was during this time that Gordon Sumner dropped the name he was never really comfortable with to become the "Sting" we know and love. Everyone in the Jazzmen had a nickname, so when Gordon showed up one day for rehearsal wearing the now legendary black-and-yellow striped sweatshirt, Phoenix trombonist Gordon Soloman was heard to mutter, "He looks like a wasp...or a bee...ahhh, Sting!" The moniker stuck.

The Jazzmen played New Orleans standards by Louis Armstrong and ballads designed to appeal to their working-class audience. Sting, happy and having fun, continued to refine his craft and pick up experience. He was almost as content as he had been as a teen, sitting on the porch with his father, playing guitar duets.

Sting began to establish a reputation in northeast England jazz circles and was invited to join Newcastle's leading traditional jazz band, the Riverside Men. Group members all wore blue suits and had been together for almost twenty years. Sting loved it. He'd joke that the suits were just as old, but he found playing vintage big band jazz very exciting.

"I was conscious of serving an apprenticeship," he said. "I learned to read music and worked hard practicing every day."

Meanwhile Sting taught at a primary school by day in addition to his nighttime jazz, and earned a double salary in the process. He was able to live pretty comfortably, with a brand-new car to boot. Sting always credited his teaching experience with enabling him to be able "to entertain delinquents for a couple of hours" onstage as a rock star. It gave him the confidence to stand up in front of people and be himself, creating an atmosphere "where people can feel happy and want to learn things," he said, explaining his comparison of teaching to playing in a rock band.

While working at Saint Paul's Roman Catholic First School in a small mining village north of Newcastle, Sting was asked to join the Newcastle Big Band, a well-known local group that played throughout Europe. At first, Sting would play only a few numbers while he taught himself to read music in six weeks, a shortcoming he managed to keep hidden from the rest of the sixteen members. Newcastle Big Band tackled a wide variety of music, from cover versions of Duke Ellington swing tunes to a raucous version of "Hey, Jude." They recorded a self-titled live album cut at Newcastle's University Theater and the Pau Jazz Festival in France. Two thousand copies were pressed and sold at shows. The LP, featuring the earliest recordings of Sting on bass, is now a rare collector's item.

From 1971 through 1974 Sting lived the musician's life, becoming an active member of the union against greedy club owners and managers. He continued to refine his bass playing, often practicing with his friend Gerry Richardson for up to eight to ten hours a day. He would take long breaks from his teaching job to learn the double bass, a skill Sting uses on his spikelike electric upright with the Police.

Still, Sting didn't think he'd ever turn out to be a full-time successful professional musician. He was young and had boundless energy but couldn't fail to notice every member of the Big Band had a day job. Sting began to realize that instrumental ability wasn't everything. To truly succeed in music, you had to have something else. Magic.

Sting's interests have always been varied; his attention was never confined to just music. He was a voracious reader and even became involved in Marxist politics for a while, a philosophy that seemed at odds with his own middle-class background.

After educating himself on the issues, he participated in demonstrations and protests typical of the time. Sting has since disavowed "street politics" and describes Marxism as "unworkable" but does admit to voting for the Labour party.

In 1974 Sting finally left home to share a flat with an actor friend in a student section east of Newcastle. In July he passed his teacher's exams and hooked up again with Gerry Richardson to put together their dream group: a jazz-rock fusion outfit patterned after the chops and technical skill of bands like Tony Williams's Lifetime (which featured longtime Sting idol Jack Bruce on bass), Weather Report, and Return to Forever. Sting was heavily influenced by Return to Forever bassist Stanley Clarke, whom he saw when the Newcastle Big Band once supported the group. It opened his mind up to the infinite possibilities of his instrument, as did the work of Jaco Pastorius. The impressionable youngster was drawn to their musical ability; he envied their dazzling execution.

With those high standards, Sting and Gerry formed Last Exit, with guitarist John Hedley (replaced after a year by Terry Ellis) and drummer Ronnie Pierson, whose band Sting had played in on the ocean cruise when he was seventeen. Sting continued to perform occasionally with the Newcastle Big Band until Last Exit secured a midweek residency at a tiny pub in Newcastle, the Gosforth Hotel. The group spun out Chick Corea covers mixed with soul tunes by the likes of Fleetwood Mac and Bill Withers. Sting's distinctive voice was beginning to take shape and made the group a real commercial possibility. Last Exit's weekly gigs became the talk of the town. The tiny Gosforth was jammed with patrons either boogying to the band's hot dance funk or stunned into silence by Sting's a cappella version of a love song he wrote called "I Burn for You." A star was about to rise on the horizon. Last Exit soon developed a devoted following, but much to the members' dismay, it never reached outside of their immediate area.

In the fall of 1974 Sting was the only member of Last Exit who still had a day job. A few months later the band landed a gig at the University Theater's Christmas Show, which featured a musical called *Rock Nativity*. A twenty-seven-year-old Irish girl named Frances Tomelty, daughter of a well-known English film actor Joseph Tomelty, was starring as the Virgin Mary. It was not love at first sight, but the musician finally won over the actress by serenading her on his guitar.

When the show ended its run, Frances returned to London and the pair continued to see each other by commuting on weekends. Meanwhile Last Exit was struggling. They performed with a few minor touring acts before securing a spot opening for the orchestral version of Mike Oldfield's "Tubular Bells," which, by coincidence, featured Andy Summers doing the Oldfield guitar parts. Sting and Summers crossed paths for the second time in their careers, but it would take the third time to be the charm.

That summer Last Exit played jazz festivals in France and Spain with Ella Fitzgerald and Oscar Peterson. During the San Sebastian Jazz Festival in Spain, the band performed before three thousand people and countless others on a Spanish television broadcast. But the lack of any real success was causing tension in the band as they entered Impulse Studios in Sting's hometown of Wallsend to record some demos. The studio was only a few hundred feet from his own backyard.

A single was released with two songs written by Gerry and sung by Sting, "Whispering Voices" and "Evensong." The group then put out a nine-track album on cassette, *First from Last Exit*, "because it was cheaper than vinyl." The songs included six written by Sting, including "We Got Something," "Carrion Prince," "On This Train," "Oh My God," "Truth Kills," and "Savage Beast." Sting also made his first foray into reggae on a song called "Put on Your Wings and Fly," which he recorded as a duet with Ronnie Pierson. He also wrote another reggae song for Last Exit, "Let Me Do It for You," but neither was ever released. Influenced by Bob Marley, Sting puts the lie to the legend he'd never heard reggae until he was in the Police.

On May 1, 1976, Sting married Frances Tomelty at Saint Oswins Roman Catholic Church in Tynemouth, in a Catholic ceremony. Sting told *Rolling Stone* in a September 1983 interview that he could never quite escape his religious upbringing.

"In the rock world, which is hedonistic and, on the surface, very existential, it sets you apart to have had an upbringing rooted in magic and religion. I'm not a devout Catholic and I don't go to mass, but I'm not so sure I've broken away from it. I still believe in a heaven and hell, mortal sins—all that's inside my psyche and I don't think will ever come out. I think human psychology is such that we invent gods and demons anyway, and the Catholic ones are tried and tested archetypes. The ones we invent for ourselves are so much more dangerous."

Shortly after the wedding, Frances became pregnant and Sting was faced with the responsibilities of fatherhood. A crucial change came over him: He became even more ambitious and competitive than ever.

"You're either the best or you're not," he has said. "I didn't want to be part of the pyramid. I wanted to be on the top. I like to be the best. I only want to be the best. I enjoy being the best. I am an egoist. I wouldn't get on stage and do what I do if I wasn't. I'm supremely self-confident about everything I do."

During her pregnancy, putting her acting career on temporary hold, Frances turned to promoting the band, bringing the group's demos to British record company a & r people. She also advised Sting on his stage presence, telling him to be more direct and less active onstage. A label rep at the time recalls traveling up to Newcastle to check out Last Exit and hearing about the group from the supportive Tomelty. His impression was that the charismatic stage presence of Sting was being stifled by the furious riffing of his cohorts.

The band continued to struggle, and Sting took advantage of the strife to take control. His abilities as a singer and songwriter, as well as his charm, were making him the center of attention. Under his direction, the group moved into an increasingly pop direction. Sting was listening to female jazz singers like Cleo Laine and Flora Purim for phrasing ideas, developing the range of his natural tenor. McCartney, of course, remained his role model. "I loved voices like his," he recalled. "I never felt embarrassed about it, either. It just cuts through everything, no matter how loud the music is...."

Finally having his own voice heard above the fusion jams of Last Exit, Sting came into his own. In the summer of 1976, in the midst of Frances's pregnancy, Sting resigned from his teaching position at Saint Paul's. He marked his transition to professional musician status with his composition, "Don't Give up Your Daytime Job." On November 23, 1976, Sting and Frances became the proud parents of a baby boy, named Joseph after her actor father. Sting reacted to the event with typical drive. He began to write more songs for Last Exit, some of which would eventually find their way to the Police.

"Daytime Job" was borne out of his frustration at being shut out by the music establishment, a feeling he claimed to share with the nascent punk-rock movement and bands like the Sex Pistols and the Clash. "The Bed's Too Big without You" and "So Lonely," which he later adapted for the Police, were both written for Last Exit during this period. "Bring on The Night," which appeared on *Reggatta de Blanc*, came from "Carrion Prince," based on a

Ted Hughes poem about Pontius Pilate and which originally appeared on Last Exit's nine-track cassette. Another Hughes poem, "Truth Kills," reportedly served as the idea for the Last Exit song of the same name, which eventually became "Truth Hits Everybody" from *Outlandos D'Amour*.

Although record companies continued to show little interest in his band, Sting managed to ink a publishing deal as a songwriter. At the time it made him feel as if he were getting recognition as a professional in his field, but the hastily signed agreement would one day come back to haunt him.

Sting's publishers helped get Last Exit a showcase at London's Dingwall's, where *Sounds*, an English music weekly, gave the band an enthusiastic review. Sting wanted the other band members to move to London from Newcastle to pursue leads. They played a batch of support shows at pubs in and around London, but no record companies were biting. And so Last Exit announced plans for a farewell gig to be held at Newcastle's University Theater on January 6, 1977.

STEWART FORMS THE POLICE: LOOKING FOR THE PERFECT BEAT

"I'm very American. I'm loud and obnoxious and I believe that you get what you deserve and work for—which is the basic American way of thinking."
—Stewart Copeland, in a *Melody Maker* supplement, December 1983.

*I*f Sting is the face of the Police and Andy Summers the Flesh and Blood, then drummer Stewart Copeland is the band's Heart and Soul. It was Stewart's irrepressible and boundless energy that kept the spark burning when the group initially sputtered. It was he who had the initial idea of the Police, a streamlined rock 'n' roll group to cut through the slick, increasingly bland music created by the progressive musical dinosaurs. Copeland was in just such a band, called Curved Air. After a particularly depressing show in Newcastle one December night, Stewart was dragged to a local college for a show by local raves, a band called Last Exit. Copeland was none too impressed.

"It was a terrible gig," recalled Stewart. "The band was a sort of sophisto Newcastle Chick Corea affair. Everyone was in their mid-thirties and balding and taking it all very seriously. And the numbers were all seven minutes long and very 'intense.' They'd moved the venue from a small hall to a small classroom and everybody was standing at this bar wondering where the band was supposed to play. There was no stage and two reading lamps on a desk comprised the light show. Everytime someone

27

walked into the room you could hear footsteps echo-
ing. . . .

"But the band went down a storm. Just because of
Sting. His singing and presence shone out. But Sting had
then what he has now. This fantastic presence. It was
really pretty obvious that he had enormous potential."

That realization would change both Stewart's and
Sting's lives forever.

Stewart Armstrong Copeland was born in Alexandria,
Virginia, on July 16, 1952, the youngest of four children;
Miles Axe Copeland III, now manager of the Police and
Chairman of IRS Records, was born in London in 1944;
Leonora, was born in America in 1946, and Ian, now head
of the rock booking agency FBI, was born in Damascus,
Syria, in 1949. Their mother, Lorraine, an archeologist,
was the daughter of a doctor and a Scottish opera singer.
Their father, Miles Copeland, Jr., was the son of a liberal-
minded Birmingham, Alabama, M.D. who had run away
from home in the thirties to join a jazz band as a trumpet
player. His subsequent life reads like a global adventure
story, and it had a large effect on his three sons.

Before World War II, Miles Copeland, Jr., was a highly
respected jazz trumpeter who had played alongside the
likes of Woody Herman and Glenn Miller. When the war
came, Miles had to temporarily give up his burgeoning
musical career to join the army, where he found himself
planning secret operations in Europe as part of Eisen-
hower's London staff. In England he met and married
Lorraine; Miles III was born in the middle of blitz-torn
London.

After the war Miles, Junior, put his intelligence training
to use by joining the fledgling American operation known
as the CIA, which he was instrumental in establishing.
He became a field officer in Damascus, Syria, where Ian
was born.

The family moved back to the States, where a U.S. senator helped Miles, Junior, secure another intelligence position in Washington, D.C. He lived outside of the capital in Virginia, where Stewart was born. Within a year Stewart's father was assigned to Cairo to help set up a secret intelligence force for just-elected President Nassar. The Egyptian leader was a frequent guest at the Copeland house, and his bodyguard even lived next door. Young Miles III would often go over to play with the guard's machine-guns; little did he know that almost thirty years later he would call on this man to let the Police's equipment cross the border so that the group could play an important concert there.

After Cairo, Miles, Junior, again returned to America, where he began his own agency, which provided diplomatic services to large U.S. corporations. His son Miles III absorbed his father's strategy in guiding the Police to international success in countries not ordinarily associated with rock 'n' roll like India, Egypt, Mexico, and Greece.

In 1957 the family settled in Beirut, Lebanon, and lived there for ten years. From the age of five through fifteen, Stewart lived in a foreign country, learning how to speak fluent Arabic while growing up in a house with half a dozen servants. He'd accompany his mother on archeological digs in the Lebanese desert. He was fifteen before he saw England for the first time, eighteen before he returned to the States.

"All the time I was thinking I was American, even though I didn't know which words in my vocabulary were English and which were Arabic," he told *Creem* magazine in an April 1982 interview.

He attended the American school for a while, then the English, without ever distinguishing himself as a student. He listened to his father's collection of big band albums and heard the occasional Beatles tune on the BBC World

Service or Voice of America drifting out of his brother Miles's room. His dad would return from trips to the United States or England with hit singles by the latest pop groups. Stewart particularly liked the instrumental hits of the Shadows (U.K. pop singer Cliff Richard's backup group), who had a series of popular tunes in the early sixties.

Miles adopted his dad's hard-line conservatism but none of his musical abilities, which disappointed the elder Copeland. Try as he might, young Miles just could not master the trumpet. As for Ian, he was the black sheep of the family, taking to hanging out with Beirut's biker gangs, who nicknamed him "Jodang," which meant "little rat" in Arabic. Ian eventually left Lebanon to settle in an outer London suburb with his motorcycle buddies.

Miles, meanwhile, developed a keen financial sense. When he was left in charge, he took cuts out of the allowances of his brothers and sisters and used the proceeds to play the stock market, building up "a nice little wad," some of which would help to pay for Stewart's college education.

Stewart must have had a hard time being overshadowed by his two notorious brothers. In Beirut he took a backseat to rambunctious brother Ian; later on, in London, he would be known as Miles's younger sibling. He was pretty much a loner until he picked up the drums at age thirteen—his brother Ian had borrowed a friend's kit but soon gave it up. Stewart, stirred by the heavy metal beat of the Kinks' "You Really Got Me," a 1964 hit, stepped right in and found himself at home.

His father, delighted that at least one of his children had shown musical ability, sent Stewart to a variety of tutors to help him refine his craft. For most of the next ten years, Stewart steadfastly practiced his drums, alone, hour after hour.

His first performance was at a nearby American beach

club, where the preteen sons and daughters of local dip-
lomats would party the night away like miniature versions
of their folks. When a band scheduled to perform one
night couldn't locate its drummer, they asked Stewart to
sit in. The rest is rock 'n' roll history. Drumming became
Stewart Copeland's life; he finally had something he could
do better than anybody else. His inferiority complex van-
ished, and a brash, confident exterior began to take its
place. And when older brother Miles saw Stewart take to
percussion like a duck to water, it made him realize he
wanted a career in show business, too.

In 1966, because of the political climate, Miles, Junior,
and his family were forced to flee Beirut. Fourteen-year-
old Stewart flew to London with his mother, while Miles
III remained behind to complete his master's degree in
the economics of underdevelopment at the American University in Beirut.

Upon arriving in England, Stewart discovered he spoke
Arabic better than he did English. He was sent to an
English private school for the completion of his education:
"The atmosphere was that we were all a big upper-class
family," he remembered. "And if we participated and
obeyed the prefect, one day we'd get to be one ourselves.
I was never a prefect."

While Stewart developed a taste for the polo played at
Millfield, the expensive, exclusive school he attended, his
father wrote a book entitled *The Game of Nations*, describing his early days in the CIA. Copeland went on to
write a second book, *The Real Spy World*, about advising
the agency in the early seventies.

Stewart went from cleaning stables at Millfield to playing for the polo team. In the winter he took to the upper-
class pastime of fox hunting. Still, music couldn't help
but reach him; it was 1967, the year of peace, love, and
Sergeant Pepper's Lonely Hearts Club Band, and swinging Carnaby Street, London. Stewart attended his first

concert featuring the Jimi Hendrix Experience, and it had an enormous effect on him. Ironically, the show took place at the Savile Theater in London the night its owner, Beatles' manager Brian Epstein, died.

Stewart graduated and went on to study music at Cal-Western in San Diego. He didn't feel particularly American in returning to the land of his birth for the first time since he was a baby.

"I've got an American passport, but I don't have any feeling of particular allegiance to America," he has said. "Nor to England particularly. I have allegiance to all those countries where I can travel and perhaps live, like Australia, Germany, France, Bali, Canada, England or even America."

Stewart found the atmosphere at the West Coast university stimulating. He learned how to communicate with people and his self-confidence grew. Meanwhile brothers Ian and Miles were now working together in a rock band agency/management firm in London. Ian returned a war hero from a stint in Viet Nam as a sergeant in the U.S. Army; Miles had left the university in Beirut to spend some time studying in the States. Back in England he ran into a band called Rupert's People whom he knew from Beirut.

Despite his almost total lack of experience in the music industry, Miles became the band's manager because they thought he might be good at it. What an understatement! Like his brother Stewart on the drums, Miles entered his new occupation as if he'd been promoting rock groups his entire life. He turned his back on politics to enter the world of rock 'n' roll, where he would become a master politician.

It was the early seventies period of English art rock, with technobands like Emerson, Lake, & Palmer; Yes; and Genesis at the height of their careers, headlining dates at twenty-thousand-seat arenas. Rock 'n' roll had grown

up from its humble beginnings into a large-scale industry.
The business of music turned into business, and the rebellion of the great punk wave loomed just around the
next bend.

Miles set himself up as a manager and agent, with a
roster of artists including such progressive rock staples
as Climax Blues Band, Renaissance, and Wishbone Ash.
He tried to break the U.S. market with frequent touring
and was soon running a fairly successful business, BTM
(British Talent Management), with partner John Sherry.
In 1971 Ian came home from Nam and joined his brother's
firm. The pieces of the Police puzzle were starting to fall
into place.

In 1975, while studying media communications at
Berkeley, Stewart received a call from Miles asking if he
wanted to manage Joan Armatrading, a black folk-rock
singer from Saint Kitt's in the West Indies who was about
to embark on her first U.S. tour that summer. Stewart
flew to England to meet her, and they returned to the
States together to huddle with her record company, A &
M, the same label that would eventually sign Stewart as
a member of the Police.

Stewart also undertook brief apprenticeships as a roadie
with Wishbone Ash and Renaissance, as well as a stint
as "artistic director" for one of his brother Miles's pro-
tégés, Cat Iron, a band that boasted a number of individuals who would be influential in Stewart's budding career.
Stewart would run into guitarist Mick Jacques again in
Curved Air, while fifteen-year-old drummer Kim Turner
went on to become the Police's road manager, sound man,
and, eventually, comanager. Kim was the brother of
Wishbone Ash's bassist, Martin Turner. One of artistic
director Stewart's more bizarre promotional fantasies had
the teenaged Turner marrying an eighty-year-old woman.

After touring the States with Armatrading, Stewart went
back to Berkeley, where he launched a newspaper for

tour promoters and college social-committee chairpeople, supported by record-company advertising. After a handful of issues came out, Stewart received yet another message from Miles beckoning him to London to hook up musically with a rock violinist named Darryl Way, whom Miles was managing at the time. His brother suggested the two form a group, so Stewart flew over and began jamming with Way in a rehearsal studio basement.

Darryl Way founded the progressive band called Curved Air in 1970 with lead singer Sonja Kristina, who eventually became Stewart's wife. The group played a demanding brand of neoclassical art rock. Curved Air had a hit U.K. single in "Back Street Luv," before Way left the band to form a new group, Darryl Way's Wolf, which he later broke up on the advice of his manager, Miles Copeland.

The basement rehearsals led to performances by Way and Stewart under the name Stark Naked and the Car Thieves, an inspired moniker. A financial crunch forced Darryl to reconsider reforming Curved Air for a final tour. Miles organized the shows at once, recruiting most of the original band: singer Sonja, Darryl, Francis Monkman on keyboards, and the immortal Florian Pilkington-Miksa, later to be known as Cement Mixer, on drums. Stewart became the tour manager, and the group did surprisingly good business, selling out dates and paying off their debts. Although he was frustrated at not being able to play, Stewart's stint as manager paid off when he met and hit it off immediately with Sonja Kristina.

Sonja's name comes from her Swedish mother. Born in 1949, she had a son, Sven, born in 1969 from a previous marriage. She spent a few years singing in a London production of *Hair* before being introduced to members of a band called Sisyphus. The resulting combination became Curved Air in 1970.

Since the final Curved Air tour was such a success,

Miles decided to put the band back on the road. A live album from the tour was released and sold well in England. A new lineup was put together, with the two remaining members, Darryl and Sonja, joined by bassist Phil Kohn, one-time Cat Iron guitarist Mick Jacques, and, on drums, Stewart Copeland, finally getting his chance to play in a professional band.

The new, reformed Curved Air broke in their drummer with a series of concerts in Europe. Stewart was nervous, forgetting parts and wondering when he would be fired. But things worked out, and the audiences were enthusiastic.

It's been said that Stewart began writing letters to the English music papers under assumed names, raving about Curved Air's drummer and asking what sticks he used—and he wrote the answer himself when the editors called for a response! At twenty-three, Stewart was finally in the company of musicians as an equal; he was having a grand old time and frequently invited his colleagues to jam in the music rooms he set up in his and Sonja's various homes.

Curved Air and Copeland recorded a pair of albums, *Airborne* and *Midnight Wire*, for Miles's own BTM label before internal friction caused the band to break up.

While Curved Air teetered on the brink of extinction, Miles's BTM company was also experiencing growing pains. In fact, it was threatened with bankruptcy after a number of European tours fell through, but Miles refused to liquidate. His two remaining acts were a faltering but loyal Curved Air and an unknown south London bar band named Squeeze. Forced to move into a less-expensive section of town, Miles found himself sharing office space with one Malcolm McLaren, who was creating a stir as manager of the Sex Pistols. Miles began to recognize the first inklings of what could be the next musical movement, one based on self-sufficiency and DIY—doing it yourself, rather than relying on huge record-company advances and tour support. The possibilities of making cheap records with the new punk bands seemed limitless.

During 1976, when most of this activity was going on, Stewart planned to take advantage of the punk and New Wave renaissance by starting his own group and leaving Curved Air for good. In mid-December the band played an end-of-term prom at a Newcastle technical college, where they were given a hard time about how much money they were earning.

Forgetting the hassles, Stewart accepted a reporter's offer to take him to see a local fusion outfit playing at a nearby teacher's college. Along with Sonja, Stewart went to see Last Exit, where his attention was immediately drawn to the seductive croon of the bass player, who had "that certain look." "Who is that?" Stewart asked his journalist friend.

"They call him Sting," he answered.

After Curved Air played their final show on December 23, 1976, Stewart immediately plotted his next move. All three Copeland brothers recognized the impact punk was having on the English rock scene, literally right under their noses. The 100 Club, where the Sex Pistols frequently played, was just across the street from Miles's offices. Everything was happening right around him and Miles wanted to be part of it.

He knew what the punks were talking about because he had already been through the mills himself. Stewart was experiencing the same reaction and decided to form a three-piece group for economic as well as artistic reasons. At a party to celebrate Ian's decision to move to America, Stewart heard Richard Hell's "Blank Generation" for the first time, in between the Average White Band and James Brown cuts his musician friends wanted to hear, and he realized that this new music was much closer in spirit to his own roots than his work in Curved Air had been.

"My taste in music is for loud guitar and exciting stuff," he said. "I didn't want to be just a good backbeat." He wanted something more. He came up with the name the Police before he had any people to play in the band—and almost lost it when another group tried to steal it.

Shortly after the first of the year 1977, Stewart called up the reporter who took him to the Last Exit show and got Sting's telephone number in Newcastle. He invited the bassist to join the band he was putting together. The confident Copeland thought he had convinced Sting to leave home, not realizing the bassist had been planning the move anyway, to set up club dates for Last Exit.

Having left his steady teaching job, Sting was wandering around London, crashing at the homes of friends with his wife and young son. Still committed to Last Exit, he refused to acknowledge the punk scene. He took pride in his craft and his own writing ability, but after a final gig at the Red Cow in Hammersmith, London, Last Exit called it quits for good. Sting was forced to take Stewart Copeland up on his offer.

"I have no idea how I did it, but I bamboozled this jazz musician into joining me in a punk band," Copeland told *Newsweek* in August 1983.

"I haven't much team spirit," confessed Sting to a *Time* interviewer that same month. "Relationships in a band are difficult."

But his acceptance of Stewart's offer was no accident. "I was desperate," Sting has admitted. "And that desperation counts." He also admitted that "I am fairly ruthless. If I find myself being compromised—say, within the structure of the group—if I'm dissatisfied with something, I'll fight tooth and nail until I'm in command...."

He has described it this way: "I've always said that ambition is stronger than friendship and people have been shocked by that but I actually believe it. I'm not justifying it morally; I'm just saying I think that." It would not be the first time Sting's fierce pride and ambition would dictate his strategy.

Stewart and Sting met in London for the first time on January 9, 1977. Two-thirds of the Police were in place. Stewart had somehow neglected to tell his new recruit the band didn't yet have a lead guitarist.

Enter Corsican-born Henry Padovani, whose parents were schoolteachers in Algeria. He studied economics in France, where he was turned on to the music of Jimi Hendrix, an influence he shared with Sting and Stewart. Padovani played in various bands while attending school in France, where he saw the Flaming Groovies perform in concert. He became friendly with the band and followed them to London in December 1976, where he attended Curved Air's final performance.

After a show by punk rockers the Damned at London's Roxy Club, Padovani was hooked. He wanted to play in a New Wave band. He was introduced to Stewart Copeland, who just happened to be forming such a group. Padovani agreed to shave his beard and long hair to join Stewart's fledgling band, the Police. But, even while he looked the part, Henry had trouble playing the parts, a fact noted immediately by Sting.

"I just couldn't write guitar parts for him because he couldn't play them," said Sting. "He had feel and spirit but for what I wanted he was wrong."

The band rehearsed songs Stewart had written, and Sting thought Stewart was organized because of his professional experience.

"Musically I thought Stewart's ideas were full of it," he admitted. "But the energy, the dynamism of the guy was really affecting me. I thought straight away, this is the bloke for me. He's very egocentric. Very, very energetic and very determined. He realized what was happening at places like the Roxy. He's an opportunist. Like me."

Before each rehearsal, Stewart would take the time to teach Henry the guitar parts, but Sting grew ever more frustrated.

Meanwhile, Miles Copeland was rebuilding his business in the punk mold. He set up Faulty Products, an independent company that managed New Wave bands and released records on a variety of different labels. He gave office space to the radical punkzine, *Sniffin' Glue*, and its feisty, opinionated editor, Mark P. (for Perry). He was impressed with the scene's commitment and ignored those critics who claimed he was jumping on the next trend. Miles finally found the excitement he had always sought in the music business.

Still, it would take time for Miles to realize he had the "Next Big Thing" right there, under his own nose. Sting, Stewart, and Henry had booked a recording session at the studio where Last Exit had done their demo tapes for February 12, 1977. For one hundred and fifty pounds they recorded an upbeat rocker Stewart wrote called "Fall Out" in one day. Stewart was forced to borrow sixteen hundred dollars from a friend to press two thousand copies of the single and form his own label, Illegal Records. The B side, "Nothing Achieving," is credited to S & I Copeland, Ian's only songwriting credit and one he's duly proud of. Because Henry was inexperienced, Stewart laid down the lead guitar lines on "Fall Out," while Padovani handled the rhythm parts. "I played the guitar on that," Copeland admitted to *Musician* magazine years later in December, 1981. "When we first got into the studio, Henry was nervous and couldn't get it together. He put it down anyway, but the guitar track wasn't happening, so I just said, screw it, and played it myself. I'd spent hours teaching him the song anyway."

While hanging out at Faulty Products, Stewart found

out about a U.K. tour being set up for a New York scene-
ster named Cherry Vanilla, a one-time publicist for David
Bowie who took up the New Wave call to arms and formed
her own punk band. Without record-company tour support, though, Cherry couldn't afford to bring her whole
band over to England; she needed a bass player and a
drummer. Enter Stewart, who had Miles convince her
management to let the Police play a twenty-minute opening set in exchange for the use of Sting and his brother
as the rhythm section. A deal was made, and the Police
hit the road, earning thirty dollars a night.

The two rehearsed with Vanilla for a week while Henry
tried to learn his parts. The Police's debut was at the
Newport Stowaway Club in Wales. They played a forty-
minute set made up largely of Stewart's material, including a song he'd written and recorded with Curved Air,
"Kids to Blame." A few of Sting's compositions were
included, too. Although Stewart wrote most of the material at first, Sting's prolific output was beginning to shift
the focus his way.

Next, a short tour around London, Liverpool, and Birmingham with New York punk rockers the Heartbreakers
and Wayne County and the Electric Chairs convinced
Sting the punk-rock scene was not for him.

"We enjoyed the energy, but that was about all," said
Sting. "But the thing was, we were going. We had a name
and that name was daubed on a few walls and we managed
to put a record out."

Stewart described the scene at an early gig. "Sting was
a dreadful reactionary. And it really showed in the early
days, which was one of the reasons we were never accepted by the punk elite. One of the first gigs we did was
at the Nashville. Everybody on the punk scene turned
out for it. And Sting came on and said, 'Alright, we're
going to play some punk now, which means the lyrics are
banal and the music is terrible....'" He just totally blew

it. He didn't understand what he was doing then."

"I was reactionary," admitted Sting. "It took a while for me to understand Stewart's enthusiasm. We were always a bit suspect from a fashion and faddist point of view because of our musical pasts. We craved credibility more than anything in those days; the music was secondary."

"Street credibility," Copeland said in 1979 shortly after the band could afford to ignore their lack of it, "is full of it. It's something journalists invented to pass the time of day. Anybody who claims to have street credibility is lying through his teeth."

At the time, though, Stewart in particular craved the respect accorded seminal punk groups like the Sex Pistols or the Clash. He wanted to be hip in the eye of the punk tastemakers who frequented Miles's Faulty Products suite.

The critics pointed to Stewart's Curved Air roots and Sting's jazz-rock pedigree and held the band up to ridicule. The cognoscenti, led by *Sniffin' Glue*'s Mark P., would have nothing to do with them. Even Miles Copeland kept an arm's length distance from his brother's enterprise, offering sometimes cutting criticism about the band's haircuts, dress, and music.

Stewart Copeland described his mixed feelings about the British music press in 1980. "That's the thing about the English rock writers. They actually participate in the music world. American press write good reviews about things they're enthusiastic about; they're more informative—informing their readers of what's happening. But in England they egg the groups on, sort of like a shadow cabinet. They're like the prosecution. I think it's a good thing that when a group is really successful, instead of just having a fan of the group write it up and make it easy, they really do examine everything."

In March 1977 the band toured for nine days in Holland supporting Wayne County, then appeared at a gala punk festival in Paris with Generation X (featuring lead singer Billy Idol) and the Jam. The constant touring, which would go on virtually nonstop for the next seven years, greatly improved the band and tightened its music. In Holland Sting introduced the Last Exit song "Don't Give Up Your Daytime Job," and the band prophetically attracted attention from a Dutch record label.

The Police returned to England in April to tour London, Birmingham, Plymouth, Penzance, Stafford, Swindon, Glasgow, and Dudley with Cherry Vanilla. In May "Fall Out" was released and sold a quite respectable ten thousand copies. Stewart did the whole thing himself, from designing the cover and putting the record in its sleeve to selling it door-to-door at the local record shops.

The Police hung on. Miles would offer the occasional gig when other acts canceled, with Stewart Xeroxing notices to advertise the show because there wasn't enough time or money to do anything more elaborate. As he had a wife and child to support, it was always a worry that Sting might leave. He briefly considered an offer from old pal Gerry Richardson to play in disco star Billy Ocean's backup band for two hundred dollars a week.

But Sting was becoming an important part of the Police as his songs turned up in the band's set: "Visions of the Night," "Landlord," and "Dead End Job" joined "Don't Give Up Your Daytime Job" in the playlist. Sting's voice was always rooted in everyday realities—paying the rent, making a salary—touched by the awesome wonder of the spiritual, both good and bad. His vision was becoming clearer; he merely needed the sound, the musical accompaniment, to make it soar. Of course, poor Henry bore the brunt of Sting's and Stewart's frustrations. Stewart was feeling the heat from his old progressive rock cohorts, who gave him a hard time for playing in a punk group. Like Sting's, though, Stewart's talents were blossoming, and he was just starting to fulfill his musical potential by playing like a madman to create the Police sound.

But Stewart made a definite decision to go for the loyal punk cult audience rather than trying for chart hits right away. It was a decision that allowed the band to grow and build a steady following over time, even if it did lead to problems with the press. They'd win over the media soon enough.

Despite the ever-present temptations of greener pastures, Stewart convinced Sting to remain in the band, but Henry would have to go. Shortly afterward, a solution to Stewart's dilemma arrived, though it would not be immediately apparent. Mike Howlett, a one-time bassist with the experimental group Gong (and who later went on to produce A Flock of Seagulls), asked Sting to join him in a band called Strontium 90, which was about to play a one-time Gong reunion extravaganza in Paris. Stewart's suspicions were justifiably aroused, and his paranoia was eased only slightly when Howlett asked him along as drummer. He didn't need a guitarist, so Henry was left behind. For good. Howlett already had a fellow by the name of Andy Summers for that job.

THE POLICE'S MISSING LINK: THE DISCREET CHARM OF ANDY SUMMERS

"Credibility was more important than anything when we first started because, let's face it, the music was very low-key. Another thing was that we could actually play our instruments. To be absolutely cruel about it, there wasn't much playing going on. It was crash-bang-crash with a few chords thrown in here and there. And I could play guitar, which was also regarded as a bit suspect."

—Andy Summers, in *Rock Hardware*

*A*ndy Summers was almost ten years older than the rest of the Police when he first joined the band. His arrival was just what the struggling group needed, and he immediately provided the musical glue that helped Sting reach his full potential as a song-writer and Stewart continue experimenting as a drummer. A lifelong professional musician, Andy brought some well-earned experience and a degree of craftsmanship to the band. He was able to handle the increasingly complex textures of Sting's songs, having cut his teeth on a wide range of musical idioms from traditional big band jazz to raunchy rhythm and blues, from avant-garde art rock to pop psychedelia, from Zoot Money to Neil Sedaka and Eric Burdon to Robert Wyatt. His middle-class roots provided the third point to the Police triangle, grounding both Sting's blue-collar angst and Stewart's autocratic ideals.

He was born Andrew James Somers on New Year's Eve 1942, in the midst of World War II in Blackpool, England. His father was in the Royal Air Force, and when Andy was two the family moved to Bournemouth, a coastal town in the south of England. He was one of four children, with an older brother, Tony, a younger brother, Richard, and a sister, Monica.

After the war, his dad opened a restaurant in the resort town. Andy showed an early interest in music and began taking piano lessons as a child. By the time he was a teenager, he was hanging out with his buddies and dreaming of leaving the quaint seaside gentility of Bournemouth for the bright lights and excitement of London.

Andy would listen for hours to his older brother Tony's jazz records, soaking up the influence of giants like Charlie Parker and Stan Kenton. At fourteen he received his first guitar. Like Sting, he got the instrument from an uncle and learned it while playing along to the latest hits. While studying music at school during the day, he began performing at the hotels in town at night.

Andy left school to work in a music store, but that didn't satisfy him like playing his guitar did. Every Friday he looked forward to waiting at the town's jazz club, the Blue Note, until he'd be given the chance to sit in between sets. At the Blue Note, Andy met a guy named George Bruno aka Zoot Money, a window cleaner who moonlighted as a keyboardist fronting his own rhythm-and-blues group, the Big Roll Band. George had formed the group a year before; they could play rock 'n' roll, traditional jazz, or r & b with equal facility.

Zoot took to young Andy right away, recognizing his talents on the guitar. The baby-faced Summers was sixteen years old but looked closer to twelve and was able to memorize music and call it at will. Each week Andy would turn up at the Blue Note and play with a different set of musicians; the club regulars dubbed the group the Andy Summers All Stars as an affectionate jibe at the jazz tradition. But the young guitarist was getting noticed . . . and making money. Even his parents encouraged him, since the steady hotel gig three or four nights a week was beginning to earn him a decent living. When Andy gave it up, he was succeeded by another young guitarist from Bournemouth with whom Summers would one day collaborate: King Crimson's Robert Fripp.

In fact, Bournemouth had a fair reputation as a thriving local music scene, boasting such British rock stars as Greg Lake, John Wetton, and Al Stewart. Andy would often jam with professional musicians at the local clubs. It was 1963, and the first British Invasion was poised to put England on the map as a rock 'n' roll breeding ground. Zoot invited Andy to play with him in a cabaret-styled band which performed a potpourri of pop, jazz, and r & b standards at a local country club.

It was during one of these shows that Alexis Korner, the legendary godfather of British rock 'n' roll, offered Zoot the chance to join his band, Blues Incorporated, and move to London. The late musician, along with John Mayall, had boosted the careers of a number of legendary British rock stars including Mick Jagger, Keith Richards, Brian Jones, Charlie Watts, Robert Plant, Jack Bruce, and Eric Burdon.

Zoot agreed to the deal on one condition: Korner would allow his own band to play a short set during the break in the Blues Inc. performance. Alexis gave in, and Zoot brought along Andy and drummer Colin Allen. After only a few weeks a promoter offered Zoot a spot playing full-time with his own band. A phone call brought the rest of Zoot Money's Big Roll Band from Bournemouth to London.

The Mods, a cult of British rock fans hooked on early Who and American soul music, embraced Zoot and his band immediately when the group took over for Georgie Fame at the Flamingo Club. Zoot's principal influences were James Brown, Ray Charles, Jimmy Smith, and early rhythm and blues. As a charismatically loony front man, Zoot would often climax his performance by spinning

around and dropping his trousers, an act Sting caught
when he saw the band perform in Newcastle. The kids in
their mohair sweaters would go insane, yelling for "the
Jerk" and rolling in the aisles. Everyone had a good time
at a Zoot Money and the Big Roll Band show.

The year 1964 was an exciting time to be in London.
A twenty-two-year-old Summers found himself there, with
bands like the Beatles and the Stones just starting to take
over the charts, but reality for most bands was a bit different. The Big Roll Band was playing up to thirteen shows
a week, and most of the band members were living under
one roof, sometimes in the same room, according to Andy.

Zoot's band's soul renditions entertained the black GIs
who frequented the Flamingo. The group got pretty tight
and would sometimes earn up to eight hundred dollars a
night. But the group couldn't translate the live excitement
into hit records: their only chart hit was "Big Time Op-
erators," which climbed to number twenty-five on the
British survey in summer of 1966. Zoot's outfit was beginning to sputter by 1967, faced with the end of the
r & b boom and the start of the psychedelic era.

Zoot began to get more and more eccentric. The Big
Roll Band turned into a quartet, dressed completely in
white with their equipment painted white, too. A lavish
light show and new material marked Zoot's arrival in the
Age of Aquarius. Andy Summers went right along, don-
ning flowing robes and turning into a hippie guitar player
for what became known as Dantalian's Chariot. Andy
lived with Zoot in a London pad that hosted a series of
wild parties attended by a who's who of swinging rock
music nobility: Paul McCartney, Brian Jones, the Moody
Blues, Jimi Hendrix, Pink Floyd.

The still-youthful Summers established a reputation as
a ladies' man, whose romantic exploits, it is said, formed
the basis for a character in *Groupie*, a famous roman à
clef about that era.

The evolution of the Big Roll Band into Dantalian's
Chariot left many of Zoot's old r & b fans behind. Even
though hard-core hippies didn't trust their musical met-
amorphosis, Dantalian's Chariot managed to build up a
loyal cult following playing at underground basement clubs.
Their light show, operated by two overhead oil machines,
was one of the first ever used by a rock band, predating
even Pink Floyd, Summers would later claim. Two var-
iable pulse strobe lights added to the psychedelic effects.

The group signed with CBS Records in the U.K. and
released a single, "Madman Running through the Fields,"
which became a minor hit among the flower children.
Outside of their London clique, though, the band wasn't
doing too well, and their problems culminated in April
1968, when the band was involved in an automobile accident. Their van spun off the road and turned over three
times, leaving Andy with a broken nose, hurt back, and
a stint in a hospital that forced him to leave the group.
Zoot had to break up the band, and former members moved
on to join Stone the Crows, Focus, and Fairport Con-
vention. Money himself crossed the Atlantic to join the
Animals in America.

When Summers recovered, he decided to throw in his
lot with one of the most uncompromising experimental
groups to emerge from the psychedelic era, the Soft Machine. Andy became friends with the band's drummer/
vocalist, Robert Wyatt, who turned him onto a clique of
nouveau hippies called the Canterbury Set, whose members populated groups like Soft Machine, Caravan, and
Wild Flowers. Summers joined Soft Machine in May 1968,
just in time to take part in the band's American tour as
openers for Jimi Hendrix.

It was a strange experience, as Summers recalled. "We
did one set with continuous music from start to finish.
We had a piece called 'We Did It Again,' which went on
for twenty minutes with just that line, repeating it over

and over and over. That was the whole thing, that's all
there was to it. The audience would just go completely
mad; they couldn't handle it. But we were definitely happening at the time. We were just too far ahead of ourselves. But we paved the way for a lot of things that came
after that."

After their U.S. tour, however, Soft Machine's bassist
Kevin Ayers decided the band should be a trio. Andy was
out. Ironically, Summers would play with him again when
Soft Machine broke up and Ayers went solo. In the space
of four months, Andy had seen two different groups dis-
solve. Checking into New York's Chelsea Hotel, he called
up his old pal Zoot, working Los Angeles with the Animals, and was surprised to find out that the band was in
the process of firing one of its guitarists.

Perfect timing. Summers took the next flight out to
Los Angeles to meet the band, was hired, and shared the
guitar role while filling in on bass (even though he didn't
like bands with two guitars, an opinion he carried with
him to the Police).

Eric Burdon was the last original member of the Animals in the group, renamed Eric Burdon and the New
Animals. The band now lived in California and had U.S.
hits with "San Franciscan Nights" and "Monterey." All
of a sudden Summers was living in Laurel Canyon and
was part of a world-renowned band. He and Zoot soon
took over the musical direction, carrying on as in the days
of Dantalian's Chariot.

In December 1968 they recorded a double album, *Love
Is*, which included a reworked version of Chariot's "Madman Running Through the Fields." Andy also appeared
on a pair of singles with the Animals, "Ring of Fire"
backed with "I'm an Animal" and "River Deep Mountain
High" backed with "Help Me Girl."

Andy Summers debuted onstage with Eric Burdon and
the New Animals at the Newport Pop Festival, where

they were very well received by a crowd there to see the Jefferson Airplane and the Grateful Dead. But Andy's skill made him a threat to certain egos within the group, and after an ill-fated Japanese tour, the Animals fell apart, leaving Summers out of work once more. He briefly returned to England, then settled in California to record a solo album on which he played everything but the drums. Summers shopped the record around the U.K. to no avail.

The songs betrayed Summers's own penchant for whimsical psychedelia and reflected the West Coast environment in which the album had been recorded. But after a potential record deal fell through, Summers was stranded in L.A. at the low ebb of his fortunes.

He moved in with Robin Lane, a backup singer with Neil Young, allegedly the inspiration for his "Cinnamon Girl." Within a few months they were married. For a time Andy gave up guitar and rock 'n' roll and concentrated on an acting career, appearing in various Hollywood theater groups. He enrolled at San Fernando State College, where he studied classical guitar for the next three and a half years, specializing in harmony, counterpoint, and conducting.

Andy Summers's musical influences are, as a result, almost all classical jazz guitarists, people like Django Reinhardt, Kenny Burrell, Larry Coryell, Ralph Towner, and John Abercrombie. Other admitted influences include the modern jazz label ECM Records; one of his favorites is Terje Rypda's album with drummer Jack De Johnette.

While at college Summers was barely eking out a living, earning fifteen dollars a week giving guitar lessons. He studied and practiced classical guitar almost ten hours a day, just, as on the other side of the Atlantic, Sting was putting in a full day on his bass techniques. The financial pressures soured his marriage as Andy was forced to reach back to his rock 'n' roll roots. He went out and bought an electric guitar, the first one he'd owned in three years.

With his musical rebirth came a spiritual awakening, too. He became involved with a woman named Kate while playing with a Mexicali band in East Los Angeles. He gradually undertook the process of reentering the hermetically sealed world of rock 'n' roll after the shock of living a normal life for almost four years.

He shared a house with actor Paul Michael Glaser, who played Starsky in the long-running television series "Starsky and Hutch." He tried his hand at acting again but returned to music when an offer came from an American singer/songwriter named Tim Rose who had a pair of sixties hits in "Morning Dew" and "Come Away Melinda." Andy made a few tapes with Rose designed to secure the British-sounding tunesmith a U.K. record contract, but there were no bites.

Andy decided to return to England to make a career for himself. In November 1973 he arrived in the U.K. with Kate and married her soon afterward. He rented a flat in Shepherd's Bush and ran into his old Bournemouth buddy Robert Fripp one night at a London nightclub, the Speakeasy. Fripp put Andy in touch with Mike Giles, one-time King Crimson drummer and childhood pal of Summers's who was about to go on tour with American pop singer Neil Sedaka, who had an opening for a guitarist.

Andy was so broke he couldn't afford an amplifier, but Sedaka loaned him six hundred dollars to buy one. Andy toured with the band until the summer of 1974 and even appeared on Sedaka's album *Live at The Festival Hall*.

"It was the first gig I did," remembered Andy. "You can't really hear much of me because it was recorded with the Royal Philharmonic Orchestra."

Tim Rose finally arrived in England and joined Andy to spend the rest of 1974 recording an album called *I'm the Singer*, but they were unable to form a band to support it on tour. Summers segued into a touring band that accompanied the road show of *The Rocky Horror Picture Show*, followed by a six-week stint with the latest English teenybopper idol, David Essex. The screaming girls and arena mob scenes amused Summers; little did he realize this kind of mania would be in his own future. Nineteen seventy-four had actually been a good year for Andy; he accomplished his goal to establish himself as a professional musician.

Andy now looked toward the next plateau: a permanent band he could call his own, a musical outfit in which he could make an important contribution. In January 1975 *Melody Maker* tapped him as a strong contender for Mick Taylor's just-departed role as the Rolling Stones' lead guitarist: "He's small, frail, and good-looking...would contrast with the hungry, debauched Keith Richards image and avoid upstaging Mick. A sturdy, reliable, and experienced musician, he would be able to supply the required mixture of intuition and feeling."

The Stones opted for Ron Wood, and Andy Summers hooked up with a band fronted by Kevin Coyne, an art school graduate who first led a group called Siren, where his idiosyncratic abilities resulted in a pair of U.K. albums for famous U.K. disc jockey John Peel's Dandelion label.

Coyne, Summers, and a few other musicians went into the studio to record the album *Matching Head and Feet*, an experimental art-pop LP much praised by critics that has become a cult favorite, too. Despite a unique talent, though, Coyne was too set on going against the rock 'n' roll grain to ever reach a mass audience. But Summers was impressed with his mesmerizing stage presence and worked well with Coyne. The duo cowrote "Tulip" on the album and another, "I Love Mother," for the next album, *Heartburn*. Andy's classical experience allowed him to play the complex rhythm and chord changes in Coyne's compositions, and when a few band members took off, he was able to repay past favors by getting his old buddy

Zoot Money into the group. Over the next year and a half, the band toured England and Europe nonstop. Not only was Summers recognized by his peers, but critics began to take notice of his work on guitar also. By managing to survive, he was starting to excell.

Andy's reputation as a session guitarist also grew. He played on Joan Armatrading's 1975 LP *Back to the Night*; ex–Deep Purple keyboardist Jon Lord flew him to Munich to play on an album as part of a five-piece rock band to be accompanied by a hundred-piece Hungarian orchestra. The rock sections of the LP *Sarabande* were recorded in Munich, while the orchestral parts were done in a village hall. While in Munich, Andy met the German experimental composer Eberhard Schoener, and they hit it off immediately. Schoener asked Andy to return to Germany to work on some musical projects with him. It was the start of a professional relationship that continued even after Andy joined the Police, one that kept Police members going in the early days when they were not making much money. Summers began commuting back and forth from England to Germany, splitting his time between Kevin Coyne and Eberhard Schoener.

In the fall of 1975 Summers landed a job playing the Mike Oldfield guitar parts in an orchestrated version of "Tubular Bells" being performed in Newcastle at the City Hall. Opening for the show was a local jazz-rock combo called Last Exit with a bit of a reputation and a flashy bass-playing singer who went by the unlikely name of Sting.

"I know Sting insists he blew us off stage, but I watched Last Exit for about three minutes and thought they were dreadful," said Andy.

Even with acclaim and a steady work load, Andy was frustrated. He was a respected session player, but he wanted to achieve something on his own, too. He recorded a single—a cover version of Santo and Johnny's

THE POLICE

A group portrait at left. Right: Sting emotes at center stage.

EBET ROBERTS

BARRY SCHULTZ/RETNA LTD.

Previous page: Sting, Andy, and Stewart play to the grandstands during their 1982 US tour.

Back in 1979, when the Police were still playing the US club circuit.

Below: guitarist Andy Summers shows off some high-stepping technique. Right: Andy and Sting demonstrate the Police's fabled musical teamwork.

EBET ROBERTS

LAURA LEVINE

Sting: "Every little thing
he does is magic."

Right: Sting in bathrobe. A quiet moment backstage during 1979 tour. Below: For the 1981 tour Sting changes to a black kimono to lead the band through its paces.

EBET ROBERTS

EBET ROBERTS

Above: Sting visits the Police's label, A & M Records, back in 1979, to check out record company support.

EBET ROBERTS

ADRIAN BOOT/RETNA LTD.

A professorial Sting dons wire-rim specs for this group shot.

An athletic Stewart Copeland toasts his favorite band after a particularly grueling 1981 workout.

EBET ROBERTS

Stewart, Sting, and Andy:
a portrait of the artists as
young men.

It was Stewart Copeland's persistence that convinced Sting to stay with the Police despite the band's struggles in the early days.

FRED ROBERTS

Sting goes mod on a scooter, practicing for his role as the Ace Face in *Quadrophenia.*

STAR FILE

Sting puffs on a victory cigar as Stewart's commitment pays off in worldwide success.

PAUL NATKIN/PHOTO RESERVE

Below: Andy Summers exchanges his guitar for a camera, signing copies of Throb, his book of photographs, in fall 1983. It was the unique guitar sound of Andy Summers that allowed Sting to begin writing more ambitious songs for the Police.

LAURA LEVINE

BARRY KING/STAR FILE

LAURA LEVINE

Sting's fierce ambition stemmed from a desire to escape his working-class background. His early love songs were in direct contrast to punk's anarchy, so the Police were never really accepted as part of the British new wave in 1977.

EBET ROBERTS

EBET ROBERTS

LAURA LEVINE

Sting and Andy hit it off immediately when they first played together in Strontium 90, a makeshift band that eventually turned into the Police.

EBET ROBERTS

A mystical Andy Summers ponders the Police's bright future.

LAURA LEVINE

LAURA LEVINE

*T*he Police's mouthpiece can't get off the phone.

*D*rummer Stewart Copeland's energy and devotion nurtured the Police into one of the world's most popular rock groups.

BOB LEAFE/STAR FILE

instrumental fifties hit "Sleepwalk," with a song he'd written on the B side—and brought it to various record labels, where he was offered publishing contracts. Unlike Sting, Andy declined to sign a deal.

A few months after the "Tubular Bells" show, Summers collaborated with the orchestra's conductor, David Bedford. He played a solo on a track called "Circe's Island" for Bedford's album *The Odyssey*, accompanied by a fifteen-member girls' choir. It was a session remembered fondly by Andy.

Kevin Coyne's band split up in April 1976 after recording a pair of albums: *Heartburn* and the live *In Living Black and White*, both of which featured guitar contributions from Summers. Soon after the demise of Coyne's band, Andy and buddy Zoot tossed their hats in the ring with ex–Soft Machine bassist Kevin Ayers, joining him on the road to support his album *Yes, We Have No Mañanas, So Get Your Mañanas Today*, even though neither of them had played on it.

Andy performed with Ayers from May 1976 to May 1977, touring Europe and taking time off to record a pair of albums with Eberhard Schoener, a partnership that continued to flourish. Coincidentally, while on tour with Ayers, Summers met Stewart Copeland for the first time in Newcastle. Stewart was in town for a Curved Air performance and was introduced to Andy after their respective shows.

Andy liked his gig with Kevin Ayers. He was on a healthy retainer and got to hang out with his friend Zoot. Kevin's manager was about to push him into the big time, and though it was all rather pleasant, Andy was not fulfilled or challenged. He began to look around for the excitement of a new, creative situation . . . one he could call his own. After close to two decades in the music business, he had yet to find his niche. At thirty-five he felt the pressure of an old man in a young people's sport. Enter

Mike Howlett, the ex–Gong member turned record producer.

Andy met Howlett at a Christmas party and became friendly with him. A few months later, Howlett approached Summers about playing in a group he was putting together called Strontium 90. The band was slated to perform at a huge Gong reunion show planned for Paris. The producer was particularly excited about a bassist/singer he had hired for the band—a guy named Sting—but Andy did not make the connection to the guy who played in Last Exit.

One afternoon in early May of 1977, Andy joined Mike, Sting, and Stewart at the Virtual Earth Studios in the Swiss Cottage section of London to rehearse for the first time. Howlett started out as the bassist and vocalist for the four-man group, which would eventually metamorphose into one of the most popular rock 'n' roll bands in history. Summers went along for the bucks, which was undoubtedly the same reason the strapped-for-cash Sting and Stewart were there as well. This lineup performed twice together. The first show took place May 28 in a huge tent at the Circus Hippodrome in Paris at the Gong Reunion Festival, where ten different Gong formations played before a crowd of five thousand rapt hippies, treated to all sorts of bizarre entertainment including fire eaters and circus clowns. The second gig was on July 12 at Dingwall's, a London pub, under the name of the Elevators. The arrangement was unusual to say the least—a four-piece with two bass guitarists—but they packed an undeniable wallop. The band's set included a pair of songs which would eventually find their way into the Police's repertoire: "Dead End Job" and "Be My Girl."

Even while Strontium 90 rehearsed, Andy was taken with the fanatical enthusiasm of Stewart for his band, the Police. "You couldn't even carry on a conversation with him," recalled Andy.

Stewart still believed Howlett was after his pet project, so he did the next best thing. He snatched the group from under Howlett's nose. For Sting, though, Strontium 90 and Howlett offered him an alternative to the dead end he'd been feeling in the Police. At last here were musicians who could actually play their instruments! He was especially impressed with Andy Summers, who reminded him that a guitar had more than three chords.

When the Elevators failed to attract label interest, Andy returned to his gig with Kevin Ayers and the Police went uneasily back to a trio rejoined by Henry Padovani. Mike Howlett went on to become a much sought-after producer of groups like Berlin and A Flock of Seagulls. All that's left of Strontium 90 is a solitary single, "Nuclear Waste," on which Sting sings and Howlett plays bass.

Less than a week after returning from Paris, the Police headlined for the first time at a place called the Railway Hotel in London. A while later, they played the Marquee, where Andy Summers came down to see them and joined the band onstage for an encore. Caught up in their enthusiasm, Summers found himself wanting to join the band, despite their obviously contrived punk facade. He saw "fantastic potential" in the band but realized the guitar player wasn't cutting it. At this time the Police played hard and fast in the prescribed punk manner, often racing ahead and leaving audiences behind in the dust. Andy saw what he'd been looking for: a three-piece band that needed only his input to complete its sound.

The final transformation was about to take place. The Police as we know them were ready to begin their quest for rock's Holy Grail. For the record, Andy phoned Sting soon after he'd jammed with the band at the Marquee and insisted he be allowed to join them. Fed up with the way things had been going, Sting warily agreed. And so the stage was set. . . .

THE POLICE
COME
TOGETHER: THE
STRUGGLE FOR
SUCCESS

Just a few days after his chat with Sting, Andy fortuitously ran into Stewart in a London tubeway and invited him to have a cup of coffee and discuss the band. Andy insisted the group could be great if they only had a new guitarist—guess who. At first Stewart was suspicious. The Police didn't even have a record contract. How could a professional rock 'n' roll veteran like Summers want to give up his paying job with Kevin Ayers to join their struggling outfit? Copeland could hardly believe Summers had that kind of commitment, but he was wrong. Andy immediately called Ayers's management to cancel his weekly retainer. It was enough to convince Stewart that Andy's interest was for real.

Make no mistake about it. For Andy Summers, joining the Police represented a major gamble. He hadn't spent the better part of twenty years trying to establish his musical credibility only to blow it all by joining a punk band. He wouldn't make the same mistake that Zoot did by jumping on a hip musical trend he really didn't believe in. Or would he?

The Police represented an opportunity for Andy to step out from his position as a sideman and finally embrace his dream of being an equal part of a band. But, before he would take the leap, there was one small condition: Henry Padovani would have to go.

If Henry left, though, the Police would no longer be Stewart's band. Stewart and even Sting resisted the move somewhat because, though he was lacking great musical skills, they both liked Henry. He gave them a certain cachet on the punk scene and he was a nice guy. And Stewart didn't want to lose any more credibility from the carping New Wavesters either. He has also admitted he wasn't keen on letting Andy into the group at first but finally allowed the guitarist to talk his way in. It was, of course, a decision he wouldn't regret.

All that was left was to make the switch, which wasn't easy. The band was scheduled to appear at a prestigious French punk festival and had slated a recording session back in England immediately afterward. Andy was brought into the band, making it a foursome. The plan was to keep Padovani on until after they finished recording.

On July 25, 1977, at London's Music Machine ballroom, the Police played their first gig as a four-piece band. It was not an auspicious debut, though. The quartet's destiny was to be a trio, according to Summers.

"I'd always wanted to play in a three-piece band and at that point I'd just been playing behind people all the time and I was getting pretty frustrated with it," recalled Andy. "When I saw Sting and Stewart, I felt the three of us together would be very strong. It was what I had been looking for for ages. They just needed a guitarist and I thought I was the one."

Sting immediately appreciated the difference. "With Andy, I had somebody who was able to perform the guitar parts I wrote, which, in turn, made me more adventurous in my writing," he commented. "We could use the vitality and energy of punk at the same time as we made it more melodic and harmonic. But Andy was the key, the missing piece to the puzzle."

A few days later, on August 6, 1977, the Police played their final show as a foursome at the French punk festival.

The show featured an all-star U.K. jamboree, including the Clash, the Jam, the Damned, the Hot Rods, and Dr. Feelgood. Henry and Andy argued about an amplifier, foreshadowing the bickering that would mark their recording session with legendary Velvet Underground founder John Cale.

Cale was a wacky Welshman brought over to England to produce tracks for Squeeze's debut LP by Miles Copeland. He was picked for the task of working with the Police. It was the wrong choice. Sting resisted the heavy punk direction Cale was trying to steer the band in, while Henry regarded him as a hero. Something had to give. Henry Padovani left the band to become the guitarist with Wayne County's Electric Chairs, who were better known at that point than the Police. He went on to play with rock critic Nick Kent's Subterraneans and his own Flying Padovanis, who released their first single in the spring of 1981.

While the Police fiddled, Miles Copeland was burning up the wires, building his own indie punk empire, encouraged by the success of "Fall Out," for which the Police received their first royalty check for four hundred dollars.

"It sold purely on the strength of the cover, because of the fashion of the time," Copeland told an English journalist in 1979. "Punk was in and it was one of the first punk records—there weren't very many to choose from."

Of course, Miles saw that there were a lot more to choose from. He organized a small conglomerate of small labels, each with its own publishing company, under the Faulty Products banner. Punk records were cheap to produce and easy to sell. The labels included Step Forward, run by *Sniffin' Glue* editor Mark P. and boasting acts like the Cortinas, Chelsea, the Models, Sham 69, and the Fall. Other companies under Miles included New Bristol Records, which released the first Squeeze LP, and Spy Records, an American punk label headed by John Cale.

Even though Miles had become a punk businessman, he didn't think much of the Police. With all his activity, he didn't have time for his younger brother's band, except to criticize new member Andy Summers's suspiciously long hair and bell-bottom trousers. But the effect of Summers's recruitment was immediate. Sting started introducing some of his old Last Exit songs, and the group began to rehearse intensively.

Gradually Stewart's material was replaced by the songs Sting would be regularly bring to rehearsals. Stewart accepted the shift philosophically. He knew Sting's songs were better than his.

"One by one, Sting's songs began to come in," the drummer said. "And because he's a writer and they're really good tunes, you can't just turn them down. When Andy joined the group, it opened up new numbers of Sting's we could do, so the material got a lot more interesting and Sting started to take a lot more interest in the group."

The brand-new threesome bowed at Birmingham's Rebecca Club on August 18, 1977. They felt uneasy about posing as punks, especially when the British press caught on to their past lives, poking fun at Sting's big-band roots, Andy's avant-garde pedigree, and Stewart's art-rock background. The few gigs they were able to get dried up.

"We disappeared off the scene," recalled Stewart in 1979. "People were asking, 'What happened to The Police? Are you still together?' We'd blown all the momentum that we had and all the credibility that we did have was all gone, though at least by this time Andy had been worked into the group, because we'd had all that rehearsal time. We were in a pit and one day we just decided to load our equipment into our cars and go off."

That fall they arranged a series of dates in Holland supporting Wayne County. They piled their instruments into Andy's Citroën and drove to Rotterdam only to find there were no gigs at all. They opened for the Damned a few times, then headed to Paris to meet County, where they played before an empty club before Andy's car broke down and had to be towed back to England.

The trip to Paris was not a total loss, though. It was October 20, 1977, when Sting took a stroll through the city's famous red-light district and got the inspiration for a song he thought at first would be unsuitable for the Police. It was slow, languid, and intense, a song about a lady of the night that ached with desire, regret, and sorrow.

Roxanne...

"It's a beautiful name, with such a rich history," Sting said years later in an explanation of the song's genesis. "Roxanne was Alexander the Great's wife and Cyrano de Bergerac's girlfriend."

He wrote a great song, which single-handedly defined the Police's sound: Sting's yearning voice, Andy's spare guitar, Stewart's thudding beat, the spacious reggae atmosphere. But it had yet to pay off. The band continued to struggle while the wives and girlfriend helped pay the rent. The Sting household survived thanks to Frances's acting work, including a part that called for a mother and a baby, so young Joseph earned his keep, too. Kate Summers worked at an advertising agency, while Stewart's girlfriend Sonja began recording an album with producer Roy Thomas Baker. Stewart moonlighted reviewing drum kits for *Sounds* magazine; he even got a free set, one he still uses, for giving a favorable review. Sting turned to modeling, thanks to his wife's agent whose floor he and Frances had once slept on when they first came to London. He did ads for men's gold chains, jeans, and bras. For the last, he stared into a camera surrounded by beautiful models clad only in lingerie. During a legendary audition for Wrigley's Gum, Sting jumped on top of a table and "gobbed" on a director looking to cast a punk. Upon discovering they needed a group for the ad, he brightly suggested some guys he knew: the Police. There was only one hitch: They had to be blond. . . .

Sting was (and is) a natural blond; the redheaded Stewart was eager to comply. Only brunette Andy Summers worried what his old musician friends would think. Although they were skeptical at first, pouring on the peroxide ended up unifying the group and giving them an image.

In October help came in the form of Andy Summers's former colleague Eberhard Schoener, who asked them to come to Munich and record some tracks with his band. The assignment consisted of Stewart's rattling and shaking some percussive instruments and Sting's doing jazz vocals, leading into a series of jam sessions, but it represented some much-needed money for the band, enough to support them for the foreseeable future. They ended up recording in Germany for three weeks, with the material released in England as the *Video Flashback* album in 1979.

Back in London, they went through a succession of managers, including a schoolmate of Stewart's who took the photograph that appeared on the cover of "Fall Out" and another man who offered them a salary and studio time. Still, nothing happened. Record companies just were not interested. They were too busy signing anything in safety pins and ripped T-shirts.

The Police held out for the right deal even when no deals came their way. Although they couldn't get a live gig, "Fall Out" sold almost ten thousand copies, so they decided to record an album and release it themselves on their Illegal label.

"Fall Out" sounds little like the Police of today. The pace is frantic, Summers's churning heavy metal guitar almost drowning out Sting's wailing vocal. With the addition of Andy, the band had the confidence to once again produce themselves. They figured out an album would break even by selling five thousand copies, which didn't seem out of their grasp.

For the first time in his band's short life, Stewart asked brother Miles for a loan so they could record. The shrewd businessman agreed to lend them enough to pay the recording bills, then proceeded to work out a business arrangement with Surrey Sound, a sixteen-track studio, for a down payment of three thousand dollars. The other half would be paid when Miles sold the LP to a record company. The rest of the funds for the LP came from the money the Police had earned playing with Eberhard Schoener.

During a break for the Christmas holidays, Andy and Kate went to the States and Sting threw a huge New Year's Eve party in Stewart's empty flat, featuring the absent drummer's stereo and reggae collection. Legend has it this was Sting's introduction to the Jamaican beat, which he would incorporate into an important part of the Police sound.

"Reggae has been a part of British subculture for the past thirty years," he said. "Ever since there's been a large West Indian community in England. It's not as if reggae just suddenly appeared fresh from Jamaica. It's been in the British top twenty ever since Millie Small did 'My Boy Lollipop.'

"It was probably Bob Marley who was the touchstone between my interest in black American music and jazz. I found in reggae an interest that was bass-oriented; reggae is bass music, where the bass takes a leading role. . . . And Marley's singing had a great effect on me, a very great effect."

Sting went on to explain that he didn't listen to reggae

that much "because we've already assimilated it into our own style, our own *whiteness*, so that now we have a hybrid that has little to do with reggae."

"I like the rhythm section in reggae," Stewart Copeland told *Rolling Stone* for the band's first interview with that magazine in 1979. "But you'd never actually find the licks that people have called reggae on our records on any record out of Jamaica. It's our own concoction; call it 'honky reggae' if you like."

Shortly after the first of the year, 1978, Sting returned home to Newcastle to participate in a Last Exit reunion concert at the University Theater. The standing ovation must have given Sting some second thoughts about his decision to join the Police, but he didn't have time to look back. On January 13, 1978, the Police began recording their first album, *Outlandos D'Amour*, at Surrey Sound Studios in Leatherhead, England. The studio was owned by Nigel Gray, a one-time doctor who gave up practicing medicine for rock 'n' roll. Along with his brother Chris, the engineer on *Outlandos*, Nigel converted a small movie theater into a demo studio, which had recently been upgraded to sixteen tracks. Rates were reasonable, and the band liked the studio for its spacious rooms and natural sound.

While the sessions were going on, Miles would drop by frequently to check on his investment. Most of what he heard he thought was rubbish, and the band was discouraged.

Andy described the scene for a *Melody Maker* supplement on the group: "We were rehearsing in this awful cellar. It was freezing cold and the rehearsals were going dreadfully. I knew Sting had had the chords for 'Roxanne' for ages. I remember him playing them for me once in Paris. We weren't really getting very far with anything, so we said, 'Let's have a go at that one.' Sting had written the lyric by this time and he sang it and we messed about with the chords. We changed it around, played it backwards and thought, 'Mmmm. Not a bad song.'"

During one of his periodic trips to Surrey, Miles met "Roxanne" for the first time and was finally convinced. It was a turning point for the group. Fired with conviction now, Miles took away a tape of the song, promising some action. And when Miles promised action, it was not very far behind. He took a copy of the song to the crew at Faulty Products, and even that normally cynical bunch was impressed. "Roxanne" had hit written all over it. . . .

Miles took the song to A & M Records, where he had some contacts as a result of his management of Squeeze, who had just had a pair of hits. He convinced A & M to release "Roxanne" as a single, and the band was ecstatic. By far Miles's savviest move, though, was giving A & M the single for no front money in exchange for a higher royalty rate and a promise to release and promote the record in the United States. In this way, the Police never owed the record company money against a huge advance. It was a revolutionary way to do business, a gamble which paid off. The Police were allowed freedom of movement, and once they got moving, they were unstoppable.

Live gigs followed. In March Miles booked the Police as support band to Spirit, a psychedelic rock group from California. The bill sold out and the members of Spirit told Miles that the Police were the best band they'd seen since coming over to England. Events now moved at a rapid pace. The Police supported Spirit at London's Rainbow Theater, with Mark P.'s Alternative TV as special guests. As the tide continued to turn, Miles committed himself to managing the Police.

During this period, the band was beginning to assume an identity, an image, a shape. They continued the recording sessions for *Outlandos* at Surrey Sound under Nigel Gray's watchful eye during the first half of 1978. The acceptance of "Roxanne" spurred Sting to write its spiritual cousin, "Can't Stand Losing You." A & M felt the setup wasn't professional enough at Surrey Sound and tried to remix some of the tracks but finally had to admit the originals could not be improved on. Demos recorded early on and discarded found their way onto the B sides of later U. K. singles: "Dead End Job" ended up in back of "Can't Stand Losing You"; "Landlord" turned up as the flip of "Message in a Bottle," while an edited version of "A Sermon" later reappeared opposite "De Do Do Do De Da Da Da."

On April 7, 1978, A & M Records released "Roxanne" backed with "Peanut," another album track from the upcoming *Outlandos D'Amour* album, as the first English single. While Miles was in the States, the BBC, the only major radio station in England, banned the song, claiming it was a love song to a prostitute. The ban made the song even more notorious, but despite some amazing reviews, the BBC's refusal to give "Roxanne" airplay hurt its sales, which hovered around ten thousand copies. Still, superstars like Rod Stewart, Mick Jagger, and the rest of the Stones were taking notice. And the spare, reggae-inflected sound of the record turned ears.

"In 'Roxanne,' we jump around a lot," explained Sting. "We played standard white rock for eight bars in the chorus, then we'd follow with sixteen bars of formal reggae for the verse."

The lack of airplay for "Roxanne" caused the band's live opportunities to dry up as well. They supported the English reggae group Steel Pulse at London's Roundhouse on April 23, but when nothing else was forthcoming, they decided to once again play with Eberhard Schoener, this time for a three-week gig at his Laser Theater in Germany, a circus tent turned performance venue.

Returning to London in early June, they discovered "Roxanne" had virtually disappeared from the charts. In the interim Stewart released a solo single, "Don't Care," on his own Kryptone label under the pseudonym Klark Kent. Klark was a reaction to the direction the group was taking with Sting's material—and the fact Sting refused to sing songs written by Stewart he couldn't "identify with."

"A lot of my songs Sting won't sing and the songs of mine he will sing, he changes the words," Stewart has confessed. "We're very different people with different ways of projecting ourselves and when he expresses himself in a song, the way I write just doesn't fit him at all."

There were no hard feelings, though. When Stewart's "Don't Care" was turned down by Sting, he created an elaborate alter ego to record it. Copeland claimed the mysterious Mr. Kent first materialized in Llandyckkk, a Welsh fishing village, where, despite speaking only a thick New Orleans patois, he became a church organist.

Actually Stewart recorded "Don't Care" at Surrey, playing all the parts and, for the first time ever, singing it, too. It turned out to be a sleeper when it was released by A & M and ended up selling thirty-five thousand copies, more than the Police's debut had. Stewart kept up the ruse all the way to New York, where A & M hosted a party for Kent, at which Stewart showed up in a mask and refused to take it off. In an appearance to perform the song on the popular English TV show *Top of the Pops*, Stewart, the Police, and even Miles Copeland showed up at the studio wearing masks, effectively concealing the enigma of Klark Kent from one and all. Later on, due to some licensor pressure, Copeland was forced to change the nom de plume to Klerk Kant.

Two other important events took place in July 1978. The Police hired Kim Turner, younger brother of Wishbone Ash's Martin Turner, as their sound man. The Police's small world was about to get smaller still.

At the same time Andy purchased an echo machine for his guitar, which enabled the Police to perform their dubwise breaks onstage.

"We play with a lot of space," he said. "So the guitar comes out very clearly. Obviously, I have to consider the bass and the vocals in what I play, but as we've gotten more and more into our style, I've been able to play farther-out things around the vocal than maybe I would have at the beginning. I have to keep the song in mind, but Sting's a very flexible vocalist. He has a good ear, and if I change the chord somewhat, he can pick up on it. And, depending on the thing we're doing, if we're jamming, he can go with it."

In May 1979 he told a *Rolling Stone* reporter he thought the Police's varied musical approach would be more successful with American audiences turned off by the more extreme British punk bands of the time.

"It seems to me that maybe some of the earlier punk bands were too radical a departure from anything Americans had been listening to. Our music falls a bit easier on their ears. We're something of a crossover between hard-core punk and the more standard rock 'n' roll: not as radical as the Sex Pistols, but definitely not Boston or Foreigner either.

"We have a New Wave tag, but to me New Wave is as much a description of an attitude as anything else. We're definitely concerned with trying not to be a dinosaur. We're against inflation of the musical kind."

Little did Andy know how prophetic those words would be. Even back then the group was distancing itself from the punk pack and, despite the disappointment of "Roxanne," their record company was still behind them.

On August 15, 1978, A & M released the second U.K. single, "Can't Stand Losing You" and "Dead End Job," an early track not included on the first album. Once again a Police single got good reviews and no airplay, and this time the BBC banned the record because of its cover, a photo of Sting hanging from a noose. Interpreting the song to be about suicide, they pulled it from their playlist. Sting was suitably miffed as he told a *Melody Maker* reporter at the time, "The BBC at the moment seem to be the aribiters of poetic metaphor. The reason they won't play 'Can't Stand Losing You' was apparently because it had the word 'kill' in it. There are countless songs about suicide in the history of pop and anyway it's supposed to be tongue-in-cheek, it's not a serious song. I felt very strongly about 'Roxanne,' because that was a serious song about a real relationship. There was no dirty words in it, it wasn't a smutty song in any sense of the word. It was a real song with a real, *felt* lyric and they wouldn't play it on the grounds that it was about a prostitute."

From the very beginning, the Police were outspoken and controversial. They did things their way—take it or leave it. Luckily their belief in themselves would pay off.

The week "Can't Stand Losing You" was released, the Police finished up *Outlandos D'Amour*. A & M picked up its option to release the album. The LP's strange title, like the two that came after it, was the result of feverish middle-of-the-night bull sessions among Miles and the band.

Miles Copeland told a *Source* radio reporter that they wanted a name that would convey the band's dangerous side as well as their romantic nature. "I compared them to guerrillas, commandos of rock 'n' roll, outlaws, Outlandos. Then I thought about their other side, as lovers, and came up with the French 'amour.' We put 'em both together to come up with *Outlandos D'Amour*." He laughed. "And it stuck!"

The group delivered the finished tapes to A & M and received a check for twenty thousand dollars, more money than any of them had ever had in the bank at one time. They split it up and cruised into the Faulty office, proudly turned out in new jeans with a load of records under their arms. After their struggling for the better part of a decade, one couldn't blame the Police for believing they had, at last, arrived. Little did they realize the struggle was just getting started and bigger game awaited them: America . . . and the world.

Gigs began to come their way again with the release of the album. The Police supported Chelsea and then recorded a session for John Peel's influential Radio One program. They played the Marquee and the Rock Garden in London, two of the more popular clubs, and began to develop a small but devoted following. The music was progressing, too, in large part due to Kim Turner's mixing methods and his smart road management. Turner used Andy's echo unit on Sting's voice and Stewart's drum kit to create the group's patented layered sound.

In early September the band received another break when Sting auditioned for and won a part in *Quadrophenia*, an English movie based on the album by the Who about the U. K. youth gang wars of the mid-sixties, to be directed by Franc Roddam. The search for cast members was much publicized, with punk rockers like Johnny Rotten being considered for major roles. Sting was about to become the "Ace Face," the Brighton "wide-boy with the best mohair suit, full-length leather coat, and smartest Vespa scooter." Little did he know his face would also be on every Fleet Street tabloid.

It turned out to be the perfect part for Sting. Just the transition he needed from modeling to acting. His current U.S. film agent told *Rolling Stone* in March 1982, "Most of the people who saw him in *Quadrophenia* don't remember that he had no lines to speak. They just remember how powerfully he came across." Acting would become even more important to the fledgling star. He had that special dramatic quality from the beginning. His first English agent saw the same strain in Sting's offstage person-

ality: "He's an enigma. Never cruel, but somehow...
untouchable, perhaps. He gives you what he wants to
give."

In another stroke of brilliant timing, a "synchronous"
event that would increasingly characterize the Police's
good luck to be in the right place, finally, at the right time
Quadrophenia would be released in America just in time
to coincide with the Police's maiden tour over a year later.
The effect was a multimedia blitz that created a large buzz
about the band. The image was coming into focus, and
the music was not far behind.

But all that was still almost twelve months away. In
reality the group's first two singles stiffed on the U.K.
charts, and the American record company wasn't interested. In October, before an appearance on BBC's *Old
Grey Whistle Test*, an aerosol can exploded, almost blind-
ing Sting. Shortly afterward, the entire band temporarily
made amends with the BBC by appearing on disc jockey
Kid Jensen's radio show.

It was at this point that Miles Axe Copeland III justified
his daddy's faith in him by coming up with a global scheme
of impressive scope. The Police would tour America. It
was a simple equation, but it represented something un-
heard-of in the music business. An unknown band just
did not do a major tour with no record-company or airplay
support.

As Sting recalled in May 1979, "We came over on
Freddie Laker's budget airways, carrying our instruments
as luggage. We paid for it ourselves, without any record
company backing. We got our own gigs, hired a van and
our own equipment and, on a very low level, conducted
a tour. A & M in the States screamed, 'You're crazy!
Don't come! You'll lose a fortune, please, it's embarrassing!' From the reps up to the president they went
crazy and rushed out the album."

And that's just the way it happened, too. The van had

two rows of seats, with just enough room to carry four people and everyone's equipment. The Police were ready to conquer America.

Brother Ian Copeland was at this point working at the Paragon Agency in Macon, Georgia, where he specialized in booking southern rock bands like Charlie Daniels and Marshall Tucker on the road. Along with Miles, he had helped establish a network of clubs along the eastern seaboard where punk bands could play, then drive to the next location overnight. They set a break-even figure of two hundred dollars a night, the same the club might pay a local band to play. Now every small town in America could afford to see a genuine English New Wave band.

The Police traveled the country, blazing a path for future bands with only the three of them and jack-of-all-trades Kim Turner. By staying in double rooms at turnpike motels for twenty dollars a night, doubling up on rooms and restricting their expenses, they could actually come out ahead. Then there were the occasional five hundred dollar gigs in big cities like Boston or New York that would pay for a day off. Miles had already proven the system by taking Squeeze over during the summer. But the Police tour was the first one Miles and Ian attempted completely on their own, although they did manage to talk Paragon into putting up the money for the van. But A & M didn't contribute a penny up front, which meant the Police could remain free to do as they pleased, without going into debt to their label. Ian drove the van from Macon up to New York as the amplifiers bounced up and down in the back seat. The American Invasion was under way and life would never be the same for Sting, Stewart, and Andy. The Police were about to enter the annals of rock history.

THE POLICE BREAK OUT: BACK IN THE USA AND BEYOND...

$\mathcal{S}$ting, Andy, Stewart and Kim were not the Fab Four. When the Police flew over aboard Freddie Laker's Skytrain on October 20, 1978, and touched down at JFK clutching their equipment as carry-on luggage, they were not greeted by mobs of screaming teenagers. The irony of the situation was not lost on the group either.

This was a different era, though. You couldn't even buy a Police record in the States, except for the spare import copy of "Roxanne," which was showing surprising strength at college radio stations. In fact, the Police have freely acknowledged college radio's role in breaking the band.

Andy Summers told a reporter in 1980, "College radio is very important to us, especially the first time we came here, completely unheralded, it was the college stations that really caught on to us. We went to a lot of these stations, and they were very interested in reading about the New Wave scene in England and reggae music, because there were very few bands over here that could talk to them about that."

The band's flight was four hours late landing at the New York airport, where Miles formed a one-man welcoming committee. The guys didn't arrive until eleven at night, less than an hour from when they were scheduled to take the stage at CBGB's. They rushed to the Bowery club, plugged in, and, jet lag or not—it would have been five A.M. for them—played a full-throttle show for the appreciative, curious crowd.

The tour encompassed twenty-three shows in a little under a month, a tiring pace that took in such exotic locales as Poughkeepsie, Willimantic, Swissvale, and Centerville, as well as larger urban areas such as New York, Philadelphia, Boston, Toronto, Detroit, Cleveland, and Washington, D.C. Playing nonstop for four weeks got the band in prime condition. The music was tighter than ever, and so were the individuals.

By and large, American audiences were sympathetic, willing to give the Police the chance their English counterparts wouldn't—band members' musical histories were of no concern to Americans. Radio stations, grateful to find a punk song they could play, began to put "Roxanne" on the air.

Then there were nights like the memorable show in Poughkeepsie described by Andy Summers in his book of photographs, *Throb*: "Only four people came. There was a short debate over whether or not to play, but we said, 'Heck, let's do it. We need the practice anyway.' So, we went on, introduced the four members of the band to each other and went bananas for two hours. Later, we shared a beer together in the dressing room."

The Police played their hardest every night during that first tour, as if they had something to prove to each member of the audience who came to see them. Seeing their time in the States as a challenge, they were prepared to go to any length to succeed. A record store owner in Texas fell in love with "Roxanne" and persuaded a local disc jockey to play it; listeners began to call in requests. Another night one of the handful in the audience happened to be a program director at a nearby radio station. A & M relented to the grass roots pressure and agreed to put out "Roxanne" as a single in the States. The grueling tour ground down with a pair of sparsely attended gigs at CBGB's. *Outlandos D'Amour* came out in England the following day, November 17, 1978.

The album contained eight tunes credited to Sting and one each cowritten by Sting with Andy ("Be My Girl") and Stewart ("Peanuts"). The two singles, "Roxanne" and "Can't Stand Losing You," formed the centerpiece of the LP, but there was other, more political fare such as "Hole in My Life," "Truth Hits Everybody," and "Born in the '50s."

"I hope people don't think of us as a pious band who capitalize on a political situation," Sting said in a 1979 interview. "I don't think a pop song is a good medium for a deep political message. Actually, politics is a source of conflict in the band; we argue a lot about its role. I'm all in favor of politics in a song, but my main area of work is still pop tunes about loneliness, isolation, frustrated love . . . teenage days. Like the Beatles wrote. The Beatles are the prime inspiration for any group. They inspire the first step, standing in front of a mirror holding a tennis raquet. Songs are a good medium for any message that is simple and sometimes that message can be political."

The album combined faster, more punky material with the spacey, tribal beat and thick chords which would come to mark their later work. An early example of this latter approach is the percussive chant "Masoko Tanga," the final track on *Outlandos D'Amour*.

"It's sung in a weird language I sang when I was put under hypnosis," claimed Sting. "I got the name for it by looking in an atlas and finding a place in Africa named Masoko and another called Tanga." He continued to be master of the put-on. Years later, appearing on the *David Letterman* Show in November 1982 to promote his starring role in the movie *Brimstone and Treacle*, he joked about the first U.S. tour. "We went back to England with the lie that we had made it in America, but it was all a series of card tricks and accidents, and here I am talking to you. . . ." The line was followed by one of Sting's devilish grins, and the audience ate it up.

Stewart gave *Melody Maker* a somewhat more honest appraisal of the band's maiden American voyage. "If we'd played a city like Boston, say, as a support act at a bigger theater to several thousand people, with the record company hustling people in, giving free tickets away, people would probably have got there just in time to catch one number of our set and maybe give us a line in their review. This way, going out and doing it ourselves, we get journalists and radio people who really do care, who really are turned on to 'Roxanne' and we dominate the gig. It's our gig and I'm sure we get much better exposure because of that."

And the trio became tighter than ever. "It made a lot of difference to us," Andy Summers said. "And the more we do, the better it'll get all the time. I really love it, because it's a very fresh situation, it's still full of challenges. We're definitely on the up at the moment. It's great!"

The band returned to London to find that *Outlandos D'Amour* had received moderate reviews and was selling steadily enough to recoup its low budget. Andy became a father when Kate gave birth to a baby girl, Layla, named after the Derek and the Dominoes song, on November 19. The Police then played London's Electric Ballroom and went out on the road as support for a satiric rock band, Alberto Y Los Trios Paranoias, formed by an English rock journalist.

Alberto were the headliners, but that status changed the first night out. Over a thousand people showed up at Bath University and sang along to "Roxanne" and "Can't Stand Losing You." The reaction was the same every night: Birmingham, Sheffield, Sting's hometown of Newcastle, Glasgow, Edinburgh, Cardiff, and Plymouth. The Police were inexorably building momentum. It was the beginning of almost six straight years on the road, a grueling stretch that would turn them into the world's most popular rock band. But it also tested their physical and mental endurance.

"It's very hard actually, as a songwriter, to be on the road all the time, because you find that your life is so divorced from normal people's lives, that you feel like, 'What am I going to write about?' Getting on planes every day, hotel rooms . . . If anything I think a songwriter should take a sabbatical—work in a factory for three weeks or something, just to get back into normal life," Sting said.

But there'd be little rest for the Police, rushing headlong into stardom. At the end of December 1978, Stewart and Damned guitarist Brian James, a U.K. punk-rock star, recorded a single with soundman Kim Turner at the controls called "Ain't That a Shame," and Miles released it through Faulty Products, distributed by Illegal. Brian played bass and guitar while Stewart whacked away on the drums. More tracks were cut for an album that never came out. After the first of the year, Stewart and Kim joined James onstage at the Electric Ballroom in London for a jam. When Andy and Sting showed up unannounced, too, wide-eyed fans were treated to a spontaneous Police hoedown.

Even while things were going well, the band couldn't afford to turn down yet another moneymaking venture with Eberhard Schoener, so they returned to Germany and played some twenty dates as his band. This time, though, the Police had begun to realize their work was more important than the income Schoener provided, and these gigs marked the end of their collaboration.

The Police appeared on a Radio Luxembourg show, then played the U.K. TV series, *Rock Show*, before flying back to Munich to perform on German TV's *Scene 79*.

The massive international exposure had the effect of a mushrooming ground swell of recognition.

On February 13, 1979, they reentered the now twenty-four track Surrey Sound Studios to begin work on their second album. Their creativity had been enhanced by the nightly improvisations needed to stretch out the material.

"We never had enough songs, really," recalled Andy Summers. "We only knew about eight tunes, so we'd have to stretch it out so we could fulfill the correct amount of time and get paid at the end of the evening. It was very good for us as a band. We probably got together a lot quicker than if we'd had a lot of songs.

"When we first came to the States, we used to expand on 'Can't Stand Losing You,' by doing a bit of jamming in the middle until it gradually expanded to become a whole other piece of material. We knew when it was coming up every night and eventually, it turned into 'Reggatta de Blanc,' which went on our second album, a very unique piece." It would earn the band its first Grammy, ironically, for Best Instrumental Arrangement.

Of course, unlike *Outlandos*, the band had never played most of the tunes on *Reggatta de Blanc* live before they recorded them. The others began life as demos, refined in the studio. Because of their constant touring, as Sting said, they weren't able to write many new songs. They considered rerecording "Fall Out," their first single, then dropped the idea.

While there might not have been a quantity, what songs they did have were quality, like Sting's epic "Message in a Bottle," which contains what many people regard as Stewart's finest piece of percussion work.

"Sting had that riff for a while," claimed Andy, tracing the song's genesis.

"The song was a hit from the time I heard it in demo form," said Stewart.

"Composing is a very private thing," Sting explained.

"I don't get many of my songs from jamming. I just sit at home with a drum box. Then I add a bass part. A lot of my compositions come from guitar parts, too. 'Message in a Bottle,' that was a guitar riff. The way I write, I don't have a melody first and then fit words to it. Actually, what happens is that I write them both together. There's this *magical* moment where you have this series of chords, this progression, and suddenly the words and the music actually come together at the same time. There's no sort of welding one onto the other. There is no other melody for the chorus to 'Message in a Bottle.' It just happened at the same time, so in a sense, I see music and lyrics as equal."

The album was recorded in a way the Police would come to use on all their records. Each member of the band went into the studio individually and came back with song demos; the entire group then decided which songs were good enough to go on the final album.

When they got to the studio, producer Nigel Gray would help the Police get just the sound they wanted, maintaining the long silent gaps and pregnant pauses that have become the band's trademark. Backing tracks (percussion, bass) go on first, then vocals, guitar, and overdubs are added. And no more. The band kept it lean and mean, as on *Reggatta*'s "Walking on the Moon." The sounds became the content instead of mere embellishment, particularly with the guitar and percussion effects.

Recording continued amidst a personal appearance on BBC's *Rock Goes to College* (a live show at a U.K. technical college) and yet another American tour. After "Roxanne" and *Outlandos* hit the U.S. charts, the band immediately flew over for thirty days in a little over a month, including three nights at Los Angeles's Whiskey-a-Go-Go, as well as in Texas, the Midwest, Canada, and Boston.

The tour roared to a climax with two sold-out shows

at New York's industry showcase the Bottom Line and
a triumphant return to CBGB's on April 8. The jaunt
closed out with a free concert at Philadelphia's Walnut
Street Theater before a wildly enthusiastic crowd that
sang along word for word on most of the tunes. A & M,
sensing renewed American interest, rereleased "Roxanne" on the other side of the Atlantic, where it broke
the U.K. Top Thirty, peaking at number twelve. On the
strength of that, *Outlandos D'Amour* came back onto the
LP charts six months after its British release. On April
25 the Police appeared on *Top of the Pops* to perform
"Roxanne."

The band continued to drive itself. They hastily arranged yet another American tour, their third in a little
over a year, striking while the iron was hot and *Outlandos
D'Amour* was climbing the stateside charts. The release
of *Reggatta de Blanc* was put on temporary hold, although
the Police did introduce "Message in a Bottle" to their
set, previewing the upcoming LP. A & M continued to
mine renewed interest in the band, rereleasing "Can't Stand
Losing You" in England as well. The record peaked at
number two in early August, behind the Boomtown Rats'
"I Don't Like Mondays." "We'll get 'em next time," de-
clared a confident Stewart Copeland, and he was right.
The Police would soon be number one.

Returning from the States to a hero's welcome in the
U.K., the Police began their first headlining British tour,
supported by the Cramps, a band just recently signed to
Illegal Records. Few even realized their pair of hit singles
were actually reissues.

The first concert was at Glasgow's Apollo Theater,
where they sold out the two-thousand-six-hundred-seat
hall and had the kids singing along with virtually every
number. The kids even knew the words to Andy Summers's monologue to a rubber doll on "Be My Girl." Sum-

mers admitted that the audience participation, which has become a tradition at Police concerts, "grows out of Sting's laziness. He's a lazy man actually, although he's hard-working. He likes to stand there, but he works hard at making them sing. We go out to the front of the stage, which excites the audience, and accompany them. You get 10,000 people singing a very simple chant, and you just stand there and play for them. It's a great feeling."

After the show, a mob of fans chased the Police's limousine through the Glasgow streets for six miles back to the band's hotel. The group had arrived as full-fledged rock 'n' roll stars.

Outlandos D'Amour went gold in the U.K., representing sales of over a hundred thousand copies, and the band was off to Europe for a series of headlining performances. Sting was here, there, and everywhere, judging the final of the 1979 *Melody Maker* Rock Contest, reviewing new singles on the BBC program *Roundtable*, appearing on BBC-TV's *Juke Box Jury* show. In August, the band marked the rise to the top by headlining the bill at the annual three-day Reading Festival in front of twenty thousand people. The acceleration of their career was dizzying, the momentum inexorable. Later that month they finished *Reggatta de Blanc*, and *Quadrophenia* opened, the movie in which Sting played Ace Face, the Brighton Beach bellboy. This double dose had Sting staring out from the cover of practically every English tabloid and magazine.

Sting told the press he had no trouble with the character in the film because it was akin to playing himself. Critics compared him to James Dean and pointed to his smoldering sensuality and quiet charisma. The week *Quadrophenia* hit the theaters, "Message in a Bottle" hit the record racks, climbing to number one within weeks. Stewart's prophecy had come true. The triple play was completed with the release of *Reggatta de Blanc*. On October 9, 1979, the Police found themselves simultaneously on top of the album and single charts.

Because of his role in *Quadrophenia*, Sting became identified with the Mod revival, with his closely cropped blond hair, long leather jacket, and motor scooter. He had developed an almost magical—there's that word again—ability to photograph well and suddenly was on the receiving end of a deluge of film offers, virtually all of which he refused, including one from Francis Ford Coppola and one to appear as the villain in a James Bond movie. One he did accept was a cameo role as an Eddie Cochran-lovin' garage mechanic in the 1979 English feature *Radio On*, featuring the music of Ian Dury, Wreckless Eric, and Kraftwerk. His role had him sitting in a caravan singing Cochran's "Three Steps to Heaven." According to whichever version a fan may have seen, Sting also appears— or does not appear—in Malcolm McLaren's notorious documentary on the Sex Pistols, *The Great Rock 'n' Roll Swindle*.

Movies and acting continue to interest Sting. "I adore being onstage," Sting reported. "Those two hours a day make it all worth it. The rest of the time is just suspended animation." But he won't take just any role; he refuses to play the stereotypical rock star, for instance. According to David Lynch, his director in *Dune*, to be released at the end of 1984, "Sting is a brilliant, spike-haired bolt of charisma." And while Hollywood had begun to take notice, Sting was already a star in his native England. Sting just ruffled his hair, set that penetrating gaze at the camera, and . . . voila! The "Sting look."

Even as they were all the rage in the U.K., the Police were cooling down back in the U.S. It was time to embark on a two-month fall tour of the States to fan the flames once again. After a second headlining U.K. jaunt in September 1979, the Police were off on their fourth trip to

America in twelve months. Because the Police continued to operate on a low overhead and managed to stay clear of record-company debts, they found themselves earning quite a lot of money.

During their October and November tour of the United States, band members spoke to *Rolling Stone* magazine about the group's progress.

"Things are moving very fast for us now," said Andy.

"We don't conform to that old wasted rock star archetype, which is one thing we share with the punk philosophy," explained Sting. "I'd like to create a new archetype of someone who's in control, an intelligent, thinking man's rocker. I'm smart and I know what the pitfalls are. The rock star myth pleases me at the moment, but, ultimately, I don't believe in it and I'm sure I'll eventually tire of it."

But America was not quite ready to hand over the rock 'n' roll crown to Sting. "Message in a Bottle" and *Reggatta de Blanc*, unlike in England, languished at the bottom of the U.S. charts. That sobering message kept the group's feet firmly planted on the ground. On October 9, the very same day they simultaneously topped the British album and single charts, they played to five people at a club in Virginia Beach.

Reggatta de Blanc's name was the result of another one of manager Miles Copeland's brainstorms. He wanted to combine the band's flair for reggae with the word for a boat race, to come up with "Reggatta," then added the "de Blanc" as a tribute to Richard Hell's "Blank Generation," the punk anthem that served as an early inspiration to the band. It's also the French word for white, symbolizing the blue-eyed approach to soul practiced by the Police. Because the record was recorded so quickly, the band members themselves weren't sure how good it was. Sting stayed awake nights fretting over the quality of the material. With songs like Sting's "Message," "Bring on

the Night," "Walking on the Moon," and "The Bed's Too
Big without You," along with Stewart's "On Any Other
Day," and "Contact," and "Does Everyone Stare," they
didn't have to worry.

Musician magazine raved about the record at the time
of its release: "*Reggatta de Blanc* is the top of a musical
iceberg that includes white ska bands like the Specials,
Madness and Selector, heavy dub bands like Culture and
Burning Spear, reggae poets like Linton Kwesi Johnson
and Tapper Zukie and seminal purveyors of ska like Des-
mond Dekker, Justin Hines, Don Drummond and the Ska-
talites. If the Police can lead people to explore the
remarkable cultural universe of possibilities (and it undoubtedly will lead to more than that), then they have
succeeded in getting their message in a bottle heard."

Melody Maker said, "*Reggatta* is the most obvious
example of different musical backgrounds jelling to produce a unique result. This time, the music has been broken
down from the chord/bassline/drumbeat thrash of earlier
material then re-fabricated into a new and tense network."

The Police were casting off the last remaining vestiges
of the punk movement. Stewart was pleased with the
results, too. "I think *Reggatta* is a great album and it was
actually very simple to record. We hardly did any rehearsing at all for it. None of us had ever heard the tunes
we were going to play."

The next American trip went beyond the club circuit
devised by Ian Copeland just a few short years before.
Miles and Ian had proven that they could break an English
band without having the group go into hock to its record
label.

"The group maintains its freedom by not borrowing
from the record companies," Miles explained. "Why go
into debt just so you can go on tour with six tons of lighting
gear and a bunch of hangers-on?"

The U.S. tour made a stop at the all-male prison on

Terminal Island in San Pedro, California, where the Police played before a "captive" audience of nine hundred inmates. The receipts were earmarked for a fund to buy musical instruments for the prisoners. The Police would play many other free gigs for charity over the next few years. Sting, Andy, and Stewart, professionals that they are, have always been aware of their social responsibilities. They would frequently hire new, up-and-coming bands to open for them on tours, giving the groups some much-needed exposure. They continually offered support to a community of musicians, a holdover from Sting's days in the union and Stewart's open door policy at the different apartments he lived in while in London.

By this time Ian Copeland had left the Paragon Agency to form his own booking concern, dubbed, in typical official Copeland style, Frontier Booking International, or FBI. Back in the U.K., the Police were buoyed by the news that the second single to be released from *Reggatta*, "Walking on the Moon," had shot to the top of the British charts. Their first single, "Fall Out," was rereleased by Faulty and sold well enough to sneak back on the charts, too. A headlining gig at New York City's Palladium over Thanksgiving weekend, attended by a star-studded standing-room-only (SRO) crowd, coincided with the U.S. premier of *Quadrophenia*. The two events proved once and for all to the American media the Police were for real. The dual blitz had exactly the same effect in the States as it had in England the previous summer, raising the public awareness of Sting and the Police, in that order. The Ace Face's confidence was growing in leaps and bounds and so was his onstage presence, becoming ever more mesmerizing.

"The prospect of performing is terrifying to me, and a lot of time I'm almost unconscious onstage," he told an interviewer in 1979. "I just go through it, not thinking, and I believe a lot of great performing artists work the same way. To see someone performing who seems to be almost sleepwalking can be quite compelling.

"It goes beyond egoism because it doesn't have anything to do with you. It's something religious, strange, and weird. Music has the power to communicate without being understood or intellectually taken in. You simply can't set out to 'make art.' You try to enjoy yourself first. I see myself as an entertainer because that's what I do best. If I should happen to make art, it's only a side product of entertaining."

The Police's U.S. tour ended on December 1, 1979. The very next day they were in Paris, taping a TV show and cramming in another series of European dates and a dozen British shows before Christmas. At these concerts the band suddenly realized they had broken through to young teenagers, ranging in age from eleven through fifteen. Becoming teen idols must have seemed like a natural development for one-time schoolteacher Sting.

The Police were the successors to the Bay City Rollers and David Cassidy, not by choice or design but by accident. The first date of the short British tour, in Leeds on December 10, was a preview of the hysteria that would greet the band at each stop. Fainting girls were dragged out of the hall. Policemania was in full swing. The band could not believe their eyes . . . or fortune.

As Sting said: "We just wanted to be a group making Top Ten records. . . . To a lot of groups, teenyboppers are a subspecies not even to be entertained, but I disagree. If you can get past the screaming, you can take a generation with you to something else. It's a real challenge."

Left unsaid was the fact that Sting's admitted role models, the Beatles, started precisely the same way. Yeah, yeah, yeah!

The fever pitch reached its zenith when the Police played two different London venues on the same night. They traveled the quarter mile between the Hammersmith

Palais and the Odeon in an armored truck hired by Miles Copeland, with almost forty security officers to keep back the mobs of screaming fans. Thousands of them milled in the streets as the army personnel also brought in by Miles lined the route from the seated Odeon to the standing-only Palais. The Police literally stopped traffic in a London that had once ridiculed them. This tour was capped off by a sold-out show at London's Rainbow Theater.

During 1979 the band sold five million singles and two million albums worldwide. They began their fifth U.S. tour with a show at the State University of New York at Buffalo on January 20, 1980, and went on to play Cleveland, Ann Arbor, Madison, Memphis, New Orleans, Oklahoma City, Denver, Salt Lake City, Seattle, Vancouver, Portland, and Honolulu. By the end of February America had fallen for the Police.

But Miles Copeland had another idea. He took another page out of his father's international handbook with a truly unique global strategy for the Police. He wanted to attempt an honest-to-goodness worldwide tour on a scale that had never been attempted before, playing venues where no rock 'n' roll band had ever been. The result was a trip around the world in eighty days: two and a half months, taking in nineteen countries and thirty-seven cities over four continents.

Miles explained his motivation in organizing the expedition. "We always want to be in a position where we're trying something new. Because when they write the history of the next ten years of rock 'n' roll, I'd like the Police to appear in the first chapter.

"We've made so much money and costs and overheads are so low, we can afford to be adventurous. There are always gonna be problems in the world, there are always gonna be people that need help.

"And I believe the Police can be a force for constructive good in this world. The group could still be doing useful things ten to twenty years from now. The band will benefit from doing unusual things like exploring new territories. Not *financially*, perhaps. But certainly as far as the *legend* goes. And I believe the Police will be a *legendary* group."

Sting also had his eye on the band's mythic standing. "There are standard ways of conquering the world. The standard route is to play America and Europe, with an occasional sortie into Japan; then you're considered a major worldwide group. We tend to think of it in another sense: there are places that aren't necessarily rock markets, places I've always wanted to visit anyway. Why not go and play rock music?"

Like Cairo or Bombay or Athens or Milan...

The magical mystery tour got under way when the band landed in Japan on February 14, 1980.

POLICING THE
GLOBE: TODAY
YOUR LOVE,
TOMORROW THE
WORLD

*A*fter a series of seven dates in ten days throughout Japan, the Police did a pair of nights in Today's World Disco in Hong Kong before fewer than a thousand people total. While there the Police were presented with the nationwide Best Album and Best Group awards in a ceremony broadcast live by satellite to British television. Miles rented some old Chinese gowns and emperors' robes and posed the band with a few of the local beauties.

On the way to New Zealand for a show at Christchurch on February 29, 1980, Sting came down with a case of laryngitis that forced the band to postpone a week's worth of dates. The case of Hong Kong flu improved enough that the Police were able to resume the tour with four shows at the Capital Theater in Sydney, Australia, where Sting reportedly first got the inspiration for "Driven to Tears," which would show up on the band's next album.

He told the *New Musical Express*, "My songs are metaphors for loneliness. . . . It's like we're all here but we're totally isolated, no matter how close you are to one person or one hundred, you're always totally isolated. And I find that image compelling."

The Police played two shows at the Rang Bhavan Auditorium in Bombay, India, March 25 and 26, the first rock band to ever visit that city for a concert. The experience left its mark on the entire band, especially Sting.

"One of the best moments of my life was in Bombay, playing for an audience that had never seen rock, that had no idea how to behave toward it," he said on his return in February, 1981. "There was an incredible range of social strata there—the intelligentsia, the media, the sophisticates, kids with no arms, beggars, hippies. Throughout the show, I explained that this is dance music, please don't sit down—stand up on the seat or just dance. And by the end of the set, they *did*! They clapped in all the right places. It was quite emotional."

The Police sold out the five-thousand-seat open-air arena. Huge crowds milled around the stadium, curious about the phenomenon. When the gates were opened to alleviate the mob scene outside, thousands of untouchables stormed in while the Indian police held them off with batons.

"Western values are very materialistic," Sting explained to a reporter the following year in Mexico City. "We think poverty equals unhappiness. It doesn't necessarily mean that in India. You see more despair, *real* despair, in Birmingham, England, where the standard of living is three hundred percent higher. In India, people are dying on the street, living in cardboard boxes, but you don't see the kind of hopeless despair you'd see in any British city or in a lot of American cities. What they say is, life is cheap. And, in a way, it is, although it's a horrifying thing to agree with. Life and death—it's their religion, and they have a way of coping with it. We don't."

The experience of India wisened the Police, as it had another band over a decade ago—the Beatles, Sting's inspiration. The results could be seen on songs like "When the World Is Running Down, You Make the Best of What's Still Around," "Spirits in the Material World," "One World (Not Three)," and "Invisible Sun."

After India, it was on to Cairo, Egypt, and a show at

the American University. Unfortunately, a religious hol-
iday had prevented the Police's equipment from entering
the country, and the concert would have to be called off,
unless . . .

It was here that the Copeland family connections would
come in handy. Nasser's ex-bodyguard, who had been
the Copelands' next-door neighbor when they lived in
Cairo, turned out to be an important minister in the Egyptian government and was glad to lend a hand so that the
show could go on. The same man who once allowed a
young Stewart to play with his machine-guns made it pos-
sible for him to make music in his country.

That was not the end of the group's Egyptian adventure, though. The band still had to fly a public address
system in from Greece and borrow spotlights from the
film crew that had been following them throughout the
whole tour. This documentary, shot by Derek and Kate
Burbidge, was later released in videocassette version as
"Police around the World." The same pair also worked
on many of the band's videos as seen on MTV and in
rock clubs.

During the Cairo concert, Sting unwittingly insulted
the chief of police, who was trying to keep the crowd
seated. The official was not amused and threatened to
have Sting detained in Egypt, but the proud rocker stub-
bornly refused to apologize. The situation looked desperate until Miles found a diplomatic solution; while Sting
nodded, Miles begged forgiveness from the chief, allowing
him to salvage his honor.

The next stop was the Sporting Hall in Athens, Greece,
where the Police were the first Western rock band to play
since the Rolling Stones' ill-fated 1969 performance, which
had resulted in a riot. The five-thousand-seat hall was
jammed, with as many people outside as in. The Athens
police were summoned to try to control the crowd.

The rest of the tour covered more familiar European

territories. There was trouble in Italy when sixteen thousand people tried to fit into an arena intended for eight thousand and the riot police had to be called in to disperse the crowd with tear gas. At another Italian show, the authorities brought in the army to provide military protection for the band. The trek rounded out with shows in Barcelona, Paris, Brussels, Rotterdam, and Hanover, West Germany.

During the final German concert, Sting's voice went out, and the roadies covered for him by pulling the plug in the middle of "Roxanne." While the crew pretended to look for what went wrong, the band drove away.

On April 21, 1980, the Police returned to England and officially closed out the world tour with a pair of homecoming concerts for Sting in Newcastle, where they donated all the proceeds to an association of English boys' clubs. The severe British tax laws had made it impossible for the band to make any money playing live, so they formed their own charity, called the Outlandos Trust, and had it run by a conservative politician out of Liverpool. The trust was set up to help young people's projects and encourage kids to learn to play by supplying musical instruments to local youth clubs.

Both Sting and Andy had to move to Ireland for tax reasons. As an American citizen, Stewart could remain in Great Britain, because he paid U.S. taxes. Aside from the home in Ireland, Sting owns one in London, while Andy bought a four-story eighteenth-century house overlooking a tiny fishing harbor in southern Ireland.

Before taking off the summer to write and record a third album, Sting jammed with his buddies Chelsea at Notre Dame Hall in London, joining them for the final three numbers, "Right to Work," "Trouble Is the Day," and "Urban Kids." He also attended the annual Music Therapy Silver Clef Luncheon, which raised seventy thousand dollars to help disabled children learn how to play musical instruments. Sting was keeping up with his social responsibilities as a rock star, as he always said he would.

It was over a year since the Police had last been in a studio. Sting retreated to his new Irish estate to write. Stewart recorded a ten-inch Klark Kent album, which was released in June.

The burdensome tax laws made it impossible for the band to work in Great Britain, so the album had to be recorded at Wisseloord Studio in Holland. On July 7 the group flew to Hilversum in the Netherlands with Surrey Sound producer Nigel Gray in tow to make their eagerly awaited third LP. The responsibility of success had made this record the most difficult yet; they were feeling the pressure from the record company—and the public—to have another string of successful hits.

The group wrestled between going off in a completely new direction or relying on the sound with which they had become identified. They tried to walk the tightrope between being experimental and being commercial. And they had only a month to write, rehearse, and produce it.

The strain wasn't eased when the Police had to interrupt this tight recording schedule to play two large open-air festivals in England and in Dublin.

The first show, a charity affair for youth organizations, was dubbed Reggatta de Bowl in honor of the Police and was held at the just-opened Milton Keynes Bowl on July 26. Support acts included Chicago rocker Skafish (who was bottled offstage), Tom Robinson's Sector 27, Squeeze, and UB40, playing to an audience ankle-deep in mud. Sting debuted his upright bass, and Miles Copeland alienated the music press by demanding that all photographers sign an agreement giving him a cut of their profits from selling the Police pix they took. It wasn't the first time Miles had infuriated the rock press, nor would it be the last, in his continuing attempts to control the Police's public image. The Police went straight from Milton Keynes to Dublin, where they played at Leixlip Castle with Squeeze, John Otway, and U-2. While onstage, Sting narrowly missed getting hit with a bottle, and during "Roxanne," Stewart was clobbered. The show was delayed until he was patched up.

All this activity made the recording of the third album a trying experience. At this stage in their career, they'd used up the store of material from their past and found that during the one time when they had most to write about, they were constantly on the road, promoting the previous two records. Such was the case with *Zenyatta Mondatta*.

Miles planned yet another world tour to start the day after the band finished recording. The sessions were exhausting. Sting experimented with several basses, including his stand-up double bass, while Andy used ten different guitars to get a wide variety of sounds. Far from home, they worked from midday to midnight, with few outside distractions.

On August 9 the Police appeared at a Belgian rock festival. In France they taped a show for the rockumentary *Urgh! A Music War*, along with dozens of other New Wave acts. Before another French concert Stewart got food poisoning and had to be replaced by his drum roadie, who kept his head down. While they played Spain and Portugal, "Don't Stand So Close to Me," the first single from *Zenyatta Mondatta*, came out and sold half a million copies during its first week of release in England, eventually climbing to number one on the U.K. charts. The album itself was released on October 3 and, despite the band's trepidations, followed the single to the top.

The group's emphasis shifted on *Zenyatta Mondatta*—the title of which, Miles told *Source* radio, resulted from his playing around with different words to describe world domination. A critic claimed it was a combination of Zen, African leader Jomo Kenyatta, and *monde*, the French word for world. In *Creem* magazine in '81, however, Andy Summers admitted, "It doesn't mean anything!"

The record reflected the band's travels to foreign lands and their exposure to different cultures. *The New York Times* responded, "The group's instrumental range has expanded considerably. Andy Summers's 'Behind My Camel' is a rather static instrumental with a Middle Eastern flavor.... Sting's 'Shadows in the Rain' includes a kind of electronic sound collage and suggests the influence of Britain's new wave of psychedelic bands. On 'Driven to Tears,' a song by Sting that might well be about India, Andy Summers contributes a wonderfully crackling guitar solo that wouldn't have sounded out of place on a Yardbirds record. Throughout the album, there's much more harmony singing than on previous records. At the same time, there's plenty of material in the more familiar Police mold, most notably the haunting "When the World Is Running Down, You Make the Best of What's Still Around.' By touring the world rather than America and by recording a new album that's pointedly eclectic and adventurous, The Police have shown that they are more interested in growth than in exploiting a winning formula."

The single was based on Sting's own experience in the classroom and his love for Vladimir Nabokov's classic novel *Lolita*, about an old man who falls in love with a twelve-year-old girl. The critics, though, pointed to the nonsense lyric of "De Do Do Do De Da Da Da" as an example of Sting and the band's frivolousness.

"I think that's one of the best lyrics Sting's ever written," Andy Summers insisted. "A lot of people confuse that, which is very annoying—like, 'he's written this baby chorus,' and they've totally taken it out of context. *This* is what is said in the verse; the chorus makes absolute sense."

Other songs, like "Driven to Tears," "Bombs Away," and "When the World Is Running Down...," expressed a pessimistic outlook about the future.

"Well, it is running down," Stewart said. "It feels that way. It feels that in the future we're gonna have to do without things we take for granted. The Third World is a reality. They can see us now that they all have televisions. They can see how we're living off the fat of what's underneath their earth. They know we're exploiting them; they want to know why haven't they got some of that good stuff. And they're gonna have to get theirs, just like we're gonna have to accommodate them."

For his part, Sting was impressed with the universal appeal of rock. Being a diehard jazzer, this surprised him.

"We played to people who have never heard that kind of music before," he told TV host David Letterman in November 1982. "And the reaction was so spontaneous, it confirmed my feeling in the form of rock 'n' roll itself."

The immediate success of *Zenyatta Mondatta* and the first single, "Don't Stand So Close to Me," did not help when it came to the critics, who remained unenthusiastic. And while the press was always skeptical of the Police, even the band members knew the recording of the album did not take place under opportune circumstances.

"This last album was a bit rushed," admitted Andy Summers. "The last night we were putting the tracks in order until four in the morning and we had to leave at eight the next day to go to Belgium to play a gig.

"We literally had to rush out of the studio, without getting a chance to really think about what we had done or see the tapes through and make sure it was right."

Nothing could stop the Police's momentum, though, not even unfavorable reviews.

"Sure, we're under close scrutiny, but we feel very strongly that we broke in England in spite of the press,"

Steward Copeland said. "They never helped us at all nor contributed to our success. We were never media darlings. We were never considered cool."

After a pair of shows in West Germany, the band was off to America once more, where mass acceptance continued to grow. They earned a total of eight Grammy nominations for *Reggatta de Blanc*, including Best Pop Vocal Group, Best Record of the Year, and Best Song of the Year ("Message in a Bottle"), as well as Best Album of the Year. Ironically, their only win was for Best Rock Instrumental Performance on the title track. It further proved the band was more than just Sting and friends. *Rolling Stone*'s poll of critics named them Best New Artist of the Year for 1980.

For this tour, the venues were more prestigious and larger, too. *Zenyatta* became the band's first-ever Top Ten record in America. A second single from the LP, "De Do Do Do De Da Da Da," was turning into their first stateside hit since "Roxanne." The group traveled to more exotic lands by doing shows in Mexico City and Buenos Aires. In Argentina soldiers with machine-guns encircled the stage, quelling any signs of enthusiasm. When Andy tripped one of the guards to prevent him from hurting someone, he was threatened with six months in jail before he meekly apologized through interpreters. The rest of the proposed South American jaunt, including a trip to Caracas, Venezuela, was canceled when Sting came down with a throat virus.

The band returned to the U.K. to play a show at Tooting Bec Common in London at the end of December. These shows were intended as a Christmas present to their fans but almost turned into a disaster when the five-thousand-seat tent erected especially for the concert became seriously overcrowded. A few people fainted, there were several minor injuries, and the British press pounced on the incident.

A Christmas show at Stafford's Bingley Hall rung out the old year successfully as the band returned to America for their most prestigious performance yet: headlining New York's Madison Square Garden before twenty thousand fans on January 10, 1981.

To everyone's surprise, the concert sold out just three days after it was announced. Andy Summers admitted to the *New York Times* that the group "approached the Garden show with a little bit of trepidation. It would have been pretty embarrassing to end up playing there for 5,000 people. But we were keen to play there and we did expect a sellout. We just didn't expect it to sell out that quickly."

He also explained how he fit into the framework of the group's live sound. "I didn't grow up on Eric Clapton and Jimi Hendrix. I always went for certain jazz guitarists and pianists, and I tried to emulate feelings I got from their music, rather than copying licks. Working with just bass, drums and a voice, in The Police, I have a lot of space; the whole harmonic area is mine. So I extend the chords and try to find new things to play. I've been playing the same relatively simple songs for several years now and there's just no end to them. I keep finding new ideas, especially on good nights. And if the crowd is there and we all feel good, then it'll be a good night."

It was more than a good night. It was magic. During their third number, a vodka bottle flew out of the stands and went right through Stewart's drum kit, forcing the band to stop the set. Sting ad-libbed while the kit was repaired and even got the audience to sing along to "The Yellow Rose of Texas." From that point on, the crowd was in the palm of the Police's hands. The show was a triumph.

"We showed our human side, and the audience had to help out, which made the room seem more intimate," commented Sting later. "Their singing made it special."

The Police continued to do things their own way. One

night after playing at the Garden, they announced a "secret" gig at the downtown, nineteen-hundred-capacity Ritz. In Los Angeles they played to fifteen thousand at the Sports Arena, only to come back the next night to perform at the eleven-hundred-seat Variety Arts Theater, requiring everyone to wear a blond wig as the price of admission. At the end of the U.S. tour, the band stopped off in Hawaii en route to shows in Japan, New Zealand, and Australia. After that it was off for a well-needed vacation break. Sting managed to get in his two favorite sports: tennis and skiing. Stewart got in some polo, and Andy went behind the lens.

After completing the Australian tour, the band returned to England. After almost three years of nonstop touring, the group had used up their ammunition for the time being.

All three stayed busy despite the hiatus from the Police. Sting played Helith, the angel of love, on the BBC film *Artemis 81*, directed by Alistair Reed. Stewart and Sonja went to Bali to study the native music, while Andy flew to India and Nepal on a photographic expedition.

Sting was also busy with solo musical projects. He recorded Bob Dylan's "I Shall Be Released" for a two hour TV feature, *Parole*, and wrote a number, "Demolition Man" (which would also appear on the Police's next album), for Grace Jones's *Nightclubbing* LP.

After three months, the band was ready to get back to work on a new album. For the first time they decided not to use Nigel Gray as producer. Meanwhile the accolades continued to pour in. *Outlandos D'Amour*, *Reggatta de Blanc*, and *Zenyatta Mondatta* all went gold in the United States. The Police also garnered another pair of Grammys in 1981 for Best Rock Performance by a Duo or Group ("Don't Stand So Close to Me") and, again, Best Rock Instrumental Performance (for Andy Summers's "Behind My Camel," on *Zenyatta Mondatta*).

On June 15, 1981, the Police began recording their fourth album at famed Beatles producer George Martin's AIR studios on the isle of Montserrat in the Caribbean, with young Hugh Padgham producing.

EVERY LITTLE
THING THEY DO
IS MAGIC

Compared to the pressure of *Zenyatta Mondatta*, *Ghost in the Machine* went smoothly, taking a little over five weeks to record. The sound was richer and more substantial than they'd ever achieved on disc before.

"We wanted to get a big, live drum sound," Andy Summers said. "There was a house next to the studio with a huge room people wandered in and out of. We took the room and put drums in it because it was a big open room with a wooden floor. The sound of the drums was great in there, instead of the studio, which was a bit dead.

"Then Sting recorded in the control room, and I virtually had the whole studio to myself all the time. I like ambience. I like the mike away from the amp and I like a bit of room sound. I had all my amps along the wall and I could play as loud as I wanted. I think all those things contributed, because in terms of overdubs, we really hadn't done any."

Another novel aspect of the album was Sting's saxophone playing on "Spirits in the Material World." "I used to play saxophone as a teenager," said Sting, "although not very seriously. The fingering has always stayed with me, and I can read music, so getting back into it was fairly simple. I'm no Charlie Parker, but it's very satisfying getting a simple riff together, then dubbing it and putting harmony on. The skills involved are fairly similar to the ones you use in singing... breathing, pitch, a sense of harmony."

In addition, Stewart Copeland played all the keyboards on the album, except for the piano part on "Every Little Thing She Does Is Magic," performed by the only outside musician ever used on a Police album, Jean Roussel.

Even the hard-to-please critics agreed that *Ghost in the Machine* represented a quantum leap forward for the Police.

"I think it's very strong," Andy Summers said. "It has a supple quality I really like, and a very positive vibe I feel was lacking on the last album. It's a true reflection of the psychological state we were in. We gave ourselves more time to record in a much better place. We basically produced ourselves with a different engineer. The whole environment was very good."

For the first time, the album's title did not have a frivolous origin, either. It was named after a book by Arthur Koestler that suggested a chemical solution for the divided houses of faith and reason in the human brain, claiming man was threatening to turn into a machine. Sting's songwriting was more pointed, more thoughtful. "Invisible Sun" was originally written about war-torn Belfast, while "Too Much Information" gently pokes fun at our media-mad universe. "Rehumanize Yourself" and "One World (Not Three)" are pleas for mutual understanding and peace.

They finished mixing *Ghost* at Le Studio in Quebec that summer. During breaks, Sting began filming the movie *Brimstone and Treacle*, his first starring role. The black comedy was written by Dennis Potter, who penned the original *Pennies from Heaven*, for the BBC, but was banned three days before it was scheduled to air. In the film version Sting played Martin Taylor, a nondescript drifter who moves in on a middle-class English family and commits havoc. Sting acted out his own angel/devil dichotomy to the hilt and admitted there was something of him in the character.

"I am as ambiguous as Martin, the character I played in *Brimstone and Treacle*," he said. "And I didn't have to delve too deeply into myself to excavate him. He's definitely an exaggerated version of me."

In September Sting appeared solo at The Secret Policeman's Other Ball, a benefit concert for Amnesty International held at the Theater Royale in London. Sting performed "Roxanne" and "Message in a Bottle" on acoustic guitar, on a bill that included Phil Collins, Jeff Beck, Eric Clapton, Sheena Easton, and Donovan. (These performances were recorded for the album from the show.) Two weeks later, Sting was performing with his old mates Chelsea as a stand-in bassist, reading the parts from notes propped up on a stool.

At the end of the month, the first singles were released from *Ghost in the Machine*. "Invisible Sun," with its potent political message, was released in the U.K., while the rest of the world got the more upbeat "Every Little Thing She Does Is Magic." The video for "Invisible Sun," which showed children playing in the streets of Belfast intercut with shots of armored cars, the British army, graffiti-covered walls, and a funeral, was banned by the BBC. The Derek Burbidge–directed clip was deemed too intense in its powerful antiwar statement. Since his wife, Frances, came from that region, Sting was especially sensitive to the situation there.

On October 2, 1981, *Ghost in the Machine* was released, and the Police began a seven-date tour of Germany. For the first time, the band hired outside musicians by adding a horn section, the New Jersey combo called Chops—Darryl Dixon, David Watson, and Marvin Daniels—who had played on many rap and funk records for the Sugarhill label, including Grandmaster Flash's "The

Message." On their return to London, Sting resumed work on *Brimstone and Treacle*.

The album was greeted as a major departure for the band. Critics were impressed with the rich harmony singing and the multiple guitar and keyboard parts.

"There was no way we could have served up another dose of what we were doing before," Sting admitted. "We had become obsessed with the idea of making marketable records. But by the time we got around to making this album, we didn't need to sell that many more records. I have confidence that this one will sell as well or better than the earlier albums, but we really did it to please ourselves. We can always return to our original sound. There's no dogma in our group, no set of rules that we have to obey, and we can hope that's true of the people who have listened to us and liked us in the past. We don't set out to be unconventional. We just use good common sense."

In December "Spirits in the Material World," the second single from the album, was released, and the band embarked on a U.K. tour highlighted by three shows at the Wembley Arena in London. After the first of the year, the Police traveled to Sweden, Denmark, Germany, Holland, and France, before beginning yet another American trip, this time at the Boston Garden on January 15. The Police would be playing twenty-thousand-seat arenas all over the States for the first time.

The band did yet another *tour de force* show at New York's Madison Square Garden on January 22, before playing February dates in Brazil and Chile. The American tour continued through March and April. Sting's second child, a daughter, Fuchsia Katherine, was born on April 17.

That May, Andy began recording a duet album, *I Advance Masked*, with his Bournemouth compatriot, guitarist Robert Fripp. The initial tracks were done for pleasure but quickly grew into a record.

"I wanted to find another guitarist to have an ongoing situation where we could work on material together outside of the group," Summers explained. "A group like the Police can get so intense that it generates claustrophobia and you lose sight of yourself as a player. It's necessary to go outside, have challenges aside from the players you're familiar with—in effect, get fresh input for the group itself."

He found the same adventurous spirit in Robert Fripp. "I wanted to play with somebody English, someone who wasn't just a straightforward heavy metal rock guitarist. I wanted someone who had a fairly wide musical vocabulary, so we could share the same kind of references and talk about it together. Robert was the obvious choice for me because I knew of his work in King Crimson. He's a guy who's made himself into a great guitar player. He's worked hard to become a technically impressive musician. He's very disciplined. I really had to adapt myself more to him than he did to me, and, in fact, I think my character is more chameleonlike than his."

He also explained how the album was made. "Every track started the same way, just two guitars. On some of them I played a little bass or put on a bit of percussion or string synthesizer. There are no drums, but you don't miss 'em. Some of it is very accessible and some is very avant-garde."

The final product was, in Andy's words, "a synthesis of two guys who grew up playing guitar, heard the Beatles, listened to jazz, have been influenced by Oriental music and Steve Reich, but still happen to be playing in a rock context."

At the same time, Stewart was filming the punkumentary *So What*! taking his trusty sixteen-millimeter camera out on the road with Chelsea, Chron Gen, Anti-Nowhere League, and the Defects.

"These are kids from urban Britain," Stewart said to David Letterman on a 1984 TV appearance. "They dye their hair pink and drop out of society. The hostile attire is to ensure that no one will hire them. Their real fear is that they'll get a job. Every week they go to the dole and collect their benefits." Behind his flippant comments, though, Stewart had a great deal of affection for the punk scene his band had managed to escape through commercial success. The movie played for a week of midnight shows at New York's Eighth Street Playhouse.

A trans-Atlantic telephone call by Francis Ford Coppola brought Stewart from England to Tulsa, Oklahoma, where Copeland agreed to write the music for the movie he was directing—*Rumble Fish*, starring Matt Dillon and Mickey Rourke.

"The voice said that Francis wanted a rhythmatist," recalled Copeland. He arrived just in time for the first day's rehearsal. "Francis said that the theme of the movie was 'time running out.' And since time and rhythm are related, he thought a rhythmatist could help him develop a concept."

After watching rehearsals, Copeland began to get a feeling for the film. "Francis wanted the sense of a clock ticking away throughout it," he said and began recording live "city" sounds in and around Tulsa. The effects— industrial machinery, traffic, construction—were then put on a repeating tape loop and integrated into an overall sound pattern for the score. Stewart composed the music around those sounds with the aid of a new gadget called a "musync," a computer that prints out the movie frame by frame. According to Copeland, this allowed extreme precision in plotting the music and working out the tempos in between.

"The project was interesting because of Coppola," he

commented. "He has an eye for spotting talent and then turning it on; he's good at generating artistic juices and he gives you a very long leash."

Copeland enlisted the aid of Wall of Voodoo singer Stan Ridgeway to create the movie's distinctive theme song, "Don't Fence Me In," later a popular MTV video incorporating scenes from the finished film.

The Police dates for July in Italy, Yugoslavia, and Hungary were postponed while Sting brought suit against the company that had signed him to the early publishing agreement while he was still in Last Exit. Sting said the agreement was inequitable and unfair. He claimed that he signed it at the time because he was broke and had a family to support.

During the court case, diaries kept by Sting recounting those early days of struggle were read aloud to show the distress he was under. The suit was settled out of court after only two weeks, with both sides claiming victory. Legal costs had already passed half a million dollars when an agreement was hastily reached.

On July 13, 1982, Stewart married his longtime girlfriend, Sonja Kristina.

There was further news on the Police domestic front when, just weeks after testifying on his behalf in the publishing dispute, Frances Tomelty, Sting's wife of seven years and mother of his two children revealed to the British press that their marriage was over. Sting began to be seen in the company of a new girlfriend, an artist/model named Trudy Styler.

In *US* magazine Miles Copeland suggested the marriage ended because Tomelty had become jealous of her husband's success. Sting explained it a bit differently. "I don't live with my wife anymore. But then I didn't live with her anyway. I was always traveling."

Frances told reporters there was no chance for reconciliation. "I want to get on with my career," said the actress, who had a huge box-office success starring opposite Peter O'Toole in a controversial British production of *Macbeth*. "You can look at me now as a single mother, not as the wife of a pop star."

Sting told *Rolling Stone* he still loved Frances. "She transformed my life and was a catalyst in my becoming something different." But Sting was changing again. In August that same magazine reported that Sting and Trudy had flown to the French Riviera for a party thrown by a Saudi arms dealer, strange behavior for someone who played a benefit for Amnesty International only the year before. Returning to the U.K. on a chartered jet, he was met by a crowd of eager photographers. A scuffle ensued as Sting sought to keep the paparazzi away from Trudy and one of the lensmen was injured.

Sting was turning into the kind of rock star he had always railed against. In September he attended a party at Abbey Road Studios with Paul and Linda McCartney to celebrate the publishing of *The Guinness Book of Five Hundred British No. 1 Hits*. Shortly afterward he admitted the Police's huge success was getting to him.

"I'm quite interested in finding me again. I used to be the same sort of person onstage that I was in private life, but now it's sort of a monster. He looks wonderful with the lights and the crowds, but in the kitchen it's a bit much. I'm just trying to find out who is the real me—is it this monstrous character or someone more normal? Right now, he's a bit worn at the edges."

August was given over to another U.S. tour, with dates in Virginia, Canada, Michigan, Tennessee, Illinois, Wisconsin, Iowa, Nebraska, Utah, California, Oregon, and Washington. On September 3 the soundtrack to *Brimstone and Treacle* came out, with Sting's version of the thirties ballad "Spread a Little Happiness" released as his first-ever solo single. The record included six Sting cuts—

the title track, the single "Narration," "Only You," "You Know I Had the Strangest Dream," and "Brimstone 2"— and three new Police songs—"How Stupid Mr. Bates," "I Burn for You," and "A Kind of Loving."

Sting was also reported to have written a screenplay based on *Gormenghast*, a fantasy trilogy by Mervyn Peake about a clever kitchen boy who tries to gain control of a castle but is undone by his sense of pride and evil. Sting, of course, would play the kitchen boy. He told *Rolling Stone* he was writing a book about his band, too. "I've got it all down, page after page of vindictive evidence. Everyone we ever met will be destroyed." He blamed the sourness on his Jesuit upbringing. "They are responsible for my venomous nature."

Both the film version of *Brimstone and Treacle* and the Andy Summers/Robert Fripp LP *I Advance Masked* came out in September, 1982. Sting was pleased his role in the movie as a demented Anti-Christ shook some people up.

"As a rock star, you find you tend to have a goody-goody image," he said. "It's nice to smash that up now and again. The one good thing that's happened to me in the last year, in terms of how I'm perceived, is that people now realize there is no goody-goody image. I'm pleased about that. I've proved that I'm a human, not a saint."

In December the band taped an appearance on the IRS-produced *Rebellious Jukebox* series, seen in the United States on cable television. Later that same month the soundtrack album to an *Animal House* spin-off movie named *Party Party* was released, featuring Sting working out on a pair of rock chestnuts, "Tutti Frutti" and "Need Your Love So Bad," produced by Dave Edmonds. Still, he was beginning to resist his role as a rocker.

"The rock rebel is defunct, meaningless, and it doesn't surprise me a bit," he said. He was quoted in *Melody*

Maker with an even stronger opinion. "I think rock 'n' roll in its highest form is a death cult. The best thing you can do in rock 'n' roll is die."

Amid the rumors the band was breaking up or that Sting would leave to pursue an acting career full-time after his rave reviews for *Brimstone*, the Police returned to Montserrat with Hugh Padgham to begin recording what would turn out to be their most ambitious album ever, *Synchronicity*. The six-week crash courses of previous LPs were put aside as the trio settled in for a long stay at AIR studios.

THE POLICE GO
FOR BROKE: THE
TRIUMPH OF
SYNCHRONICITY

"I do my best work when I'm in pain and turmoil."
—Sting, in *Rolling Stone*, September 1983

*S*till reeling over the failure of his marriage, Sting left in the middle of mixing the new album at Quebec's Le Studio to live in James Bond–author Ian Fleming's old mansion in Jamaica for a few months. He turned his hurt into his most moving love song, "Every Breath You Take."

But the song turned out to have a double edge. "I find the 'I'll-be-watching-you' motif quite frightening. Perhaps the song was a synchronistic prophecy, because as a people, we've all gotten to Orwell's 1984 a year early—the book is no longer science fiction but a sublime aggregate of the world's current atrocities. As for the song, I think it's shadowy, evil, and insidious, and the fact that it's been at the top of the American record charts proves the point. . . . People don't know what they're hearing! It's absolute poison," he said.

He explained that the record "should say to the world that we are individuals. We are not joined at the hip; we are not a three-headed Hydra. We were very much thrown together by accident and we're very distinguished by strong egos. And we each have our own contributions to make. That was brought out on the album cover, where my idea was for each of us to have a separate strip and have the freedom photographically to do whatever we as individuals wanted, without knowing what the other two had

125

planned. We'll find out when the album comes out if it's synchronistic or not. Hopefully, it will be."

When the album finally did come out, Andy and Stewart were represented by a song apiece; Sting had written the other eight. "If I have an idea I believe in, I'll kill for it, and I would hope that the others feel the same," he commented. "That's where the anger and tension come in, and it's not a bad thing. A guitar string wouldn't sound without tension; if it were all loose, it would sound terrible. So I like to pull on the strings of the group to manufacture that situation. Sometimes there are casualties."

He admitted as much to *Rolling Stone* in February 1981: "Yeah, I am fairly ruthless. I'll fight tooth and nail until I'm in command. There's no pussyfooting in our group. We don't skirt around each other; we go straight for the jugular. We know each other very well, and we know where it hurts. It's not ultimately destructive; it's ultimately creative. Friendships come second for me, as far as musical ones go.

"There's a competitive spirit in the group; there are three very strong egos. But I write and sing the songs, therefore I tend to dictate the musical direction. We do have a semblance of democracy, which is important. But the fact is, the most efficient way of running the group is to have me sing, because I'm a good singer. I perform the songs onstage. If there were another singer/songwriter in the group, I'd be relieved in many ways, actually, because it's a heavy responsibility. The other two write songs, but in their heart of hearts, they hope that Sting is going to come out with the hits, the ones that get played on the radio."

Mild-mannered Andy Summers isn't bothered by the attention commanded by Sting. "I don't envy him. I like to be anonymous actually. I like to show off onstage, and I enjoy the stardom part of it as well, but I'm glad Sting has had all that attention, because he's been a fantastic focal point. He is the frontman and the singer, and he's the perfect archetype. He has everything: the right height, the blond hair, blue eyes, a great voice, he's nice looking. He's the perfect lead man and should be used to its fullest extent."

Even in the shadow of Sting, Andy was stung by the pressure of success when his marriage to Kate broke up. He blamed the constant touring of the Police for the split and bemoaned "the emotional tightrope between being a pop star and coming home to a wife and child."

Andy poured his heart into his track on *Synchronicity*, "Mother." It was his first vocal performance since his infamous rap on "Be My Girl."

On finishing the album, Sting moved into the Château Marmont Hotel in Hollywood with his girlfriend, Trudy. "Every Breath You Take," the first single, came out at the end of May, accompanied by a stunning video shot by directors Kevin Godley and Lol Creme, members of the rock group 10cc. The clip, an homage to an old jazz film, *Jammin' the Blues*, with saxophonist Lester Young, was done in the four different monochromatic colors of the album and its attendant packaging: red, yellow, blue, and black-and-white. Each copy of the LP had a unique color scheme and a distinct arrangement of photographs randomly placed together in the "synchronous" fashion Sting had described. The record was named after the theories of psychologist C. G. Jung, dealing with the connection between different events happening in different places at the same time. It was as apt a description as any in describing the success of the three disparate individuals who came together to form the Police.

The band's sound had been imitated so widely at this point that the Police felt they had to come up with something unique. "It is important that this album be different," Sting said. "The new album is about having a personal voice. All of us got the chance to say things quietly and quite emotionally. I think these lyrics are the best I've done."

As the album was being released, Sting was off to Mexico for a role in Dino De Laurentiis's multimillion-dollar adaptation of Frank Herbert's science fiction cult classic, *Dune*, scheduled for release at Christmas 1984. Sting agreed to the part after learning that David Lynch, with the avant-garde *Eraserhead* and atmospheric *Elephant Man* to his credit, would be the director.

"Feyd-Ravtha is an heir to the Harkonnen's feudal system," he said of his alter ego in *Dune*. "His is a family of really evil, rancid people who live on this really sick planet and have terrible diseases with huge boils of pus. They are wicked. I got very partisan on the set: you're either a Harkonnen or an Atreides, who were the good guys. I hated the Atreides actors; we had separate dressing rooms. If you had to do a scene in which you were angry at them, you'd spend a half-hour beforehand telling them to get lost!"

The June 10, 1983, release of *Synchronicity* was greeted with an unprecedented enthusiasm by public and critics alike. The usually tough British *New Musical Express* called it "A record of real passion that is impossible to truly decipher." *Musician* chimed in with, "A reflective, bittersweet pop masterwork." The *New York Times* compared it with the Beatles' *Sergeant Pepper's Lonely Hearts Club Band*, which probably made Sting happiest and proudest of all.

"*Synchronicity* isn't the first album since *Sergeant Pepper* to have its finger so firmly on the pulse of the times that it manages to be genuinely avant-garde and genuinely commercial at the same time. But it doesn't happen very often, especially these days, and the fact that The Police have made it happen again is cause for rejoicing. It's an easy album to listen to, for on even a superficial level its arching melodies and unprecedented rhythmic variety are exhilarating....

"On *Synchronicity*, The Police have expanded their style in a multitude of directions, using as much of what they have learned as can sensibly be fitted on one record. And what comes out isn't a mishmash of borrowed ethnic rhythms and melodies, it's an organic, original sound....

"Sting has a gift for turning melodic phrases that recalls Paul McCartney, but the intensity and acerbity of his latest songs is more reminiscent of John Lennon. *Synchronicity* is especially welcome because it has more bite, more juice, than any previous Police LP."

Aside from the reviewers, though, *Synchronicity* turned out to be the Police's most popular album ever, a fact not lost on a populist-minded Sting. "Hit records are everything," he said. "I love making them. They're what drive the band. But making this album was a pretty painful process because we knew we had a real challenge on our hands, to change the way we play and our attitudes. For in order for a band to stay vital you have to change, which is very hard."

The Police's American tour in the summer of 1983 was a calculated gamble. Sprinkled in among the twenty-thousand-capacity sports arenas they had become accustomed to were a few sixty-thousand-seat outdoor stadiums, including Shea Stadium in New York, where the Beatles had performed their historic concert eighteen years before.

Sting responded to the bookings in mammoth stadiums in an interview with the *Record* in August 1983: "I think part of my job is creating the illusion of intimacy of a club atmosphere in some place that's massive. Working against the atmosphere is a challenge. Sometimes it can't work. Our secret is that we can entertain a lot of people without being condescending, without lowering ourselves to a common denominator that everybody can understand. I think we can be informative and fun at the same time. Those ninety minutes I'm on stage is the only joy in my life. It's my only release, my only happiness. The rest of it is awful, pure loathing."

Right before leaving on tour, Stewart and Sonja's first son, Jordan Daniel, was born on June 28, 1983. It was a good omen, a synchronous event.

The shows began before a sold-out crowd at Chicago's Comiskey Park numbering close to fifty thousand fans. MTV—Music Television, the twenty-four-hour video-music cable network, sponsored the tour in a historic arrangement, issuing live reports from the sites and promoting contests with the band. Add in the constant airplay for the different video versions of "Every Breath You Take," and the Police were increasing their already immense popularity by leaps and bounds.

"Every Breath You Take" became the first Police single to ever reach number one on the American charts, and the *Synchronicity* LP followed it to the top.

After the first show in Comiskey Park, an eager MTV reporter asked Sting what he thought of the show. "I'm advertising for a new band," he deadpanned.

"I don't want to become a reaction to people's perceptions about me," he said to a *Time* magazine reporter. "If their perceptions are all mixed up and contradictory, that's wonderful. Then I can be myself."

On the road, Sting continued to keep a daily journal, which he'd been working on since 1974. He taught himself to program his portable synthesizer and continued to work on his developing tennis game. As always, he didn't smoke, ate balanced meals, drank only in moderation, and exercised daily. He is a somewhat solitary man, with few close friends. He reveals himself in his songs.

"All my songs are about me. You are all you can write about really. It's all you can know," he has confessed.

"I think these lyrics are the best I've ever done," he also said "It's been a year of hell and torture for me . . . And I know that without that torture and without that pain, those lyrics wouldn't have been as good. So in a sense I'm very suspicious of myself. I wonder if I manufacture pain in order to create."

The emotional climax of the American portion of the *Synchronicity* tour came on August 18, 1983, before a crowd of seventy thousand fans at Shea Stadium.

"We'd like to thank the Beatles for lending us their stadium," joked Sting, but he really meant it. He had achieved the impossible and actually matched the feats of his old idols. Even Sting admitted the Police's accomplishments would be tough to top.

"The frightening thing is, The Police have reached such a point of success. Where do you take it from here? Do you just carry on? My threshold of boredom is very low. I believe in taking risks. So, I'd have to say I'm on the brink of something," he said.

Still, as he also admitted, "When someone waves a million dollars in front of your face to do something you consider fun, what do you say? You say 'yeah.' The pull is the attraction of the unknown, that nagging ambition for some kind of pure productive peace away from Sunset Boulevard and the running lackeys of the publicity mills. I don't want to be an idol. I don't want to be famous. It's a means to an end, I hope. An end I change my mind about every day."

He elaborated on his dilemma. "It's not as if we're bound together in financial brotherhood. We're all very free; the group could end tomorrow without damaging any of us. Acting certainly puts a new angle on the whole thing, more interesting than rock star tour-album-tour-album. Since acting makes me more interesting, it makes the music more interesting. It's a way to recharge the batteries without wasting any time.

"I'm not irresponsible; I'm not just gonna walk out. But if something really interests me, and I see the group standing in my way...I just don't want to keep regurgitating the same rituals. I suppose it's all part of refining myself out of existence; the songs can be there, the voice can be there, but me, I'd rather not be talking to any interviewers. I'd rather be home with my feet up."

The Police filmed their Montreal concert for a U.S. cable special but weren't pleased with the results, so they taped a show later on in the tour at the Omni in Atlanta. It was directed by Godley and Creme, who had done all their videos from the *Synchronicity* album. The show aired as *Police: the Synchronicity Concert*.

Three more singles were released from the album, including "Wrapped around Your Finger," "Synchronicity II," and "King of Pain." All but the last were accompanied by Godley and Creme-directed videos. Each made the U.S. Top Ten, and the album went way beyond the platinum mark, selling well over five million copies in the U.S. alone. Meanwhile the worldwide trek continued into Germany, France, Spain, Holland, and Sweden as 1984 approached.

In October Andy's book of photographs, *Throb*, was published. It included a lot of photos of Sting and the band in exotic locales. Summers chose all the photos and wrote all the copy. He told TV's David Letterman that "Throb is a very 'edgy' word, sort of tongue-in-cheek, with a definite sexual connotation." The book lived up to that with its revealing pix of nude women and Sting in the shower. Other photos included Stewart terrified on an airplane, Andy and his maid on Montserrat, Sting and a statue of an Indian, and someone hanging from a chandelier. Andy also said the only place he was forbidden to take pictures during the band's famous 1980 world tour was in India, where authorities confiscated his cameras as soon as they arrived because Indira Gandhi was "apparently worried about bad publicity."

December brought another British tour, with sixteen dates spread out over the course of a month, capped by four shows at Wembley. The Police didn't let up after the new year, either, heading for still more dates in Europe and Australia. On January 19, 1984, Trudy Styler gave birth to Sting's third child and second daughter, Michele Bridget.

By now the Police were indisputably the biggest and most popular rock 'n' roll band in the world. They had done what no other group since the Beatles could do. They were known in every part of the civilized world. They had attained the pinnacle of pop success. Now the question was could they stay together?

The friction and rivalry in the band which resulted in its best work also undermined its stability. As Stewart had confessed, the group could break up over the least silly thing, "like who had the extra egg at breakfast."

"It's not an easy relationship, by any means," Sting said to *Rolling Stone*. "We're three highly autonomous individuals, and a band is an artificial alliance most of the time. There are obviously tensions, but I think there's a great love between us and a genuine respect. I can't think of two musicians I'd rather play with."

He repeated the point later. "I've stopped writing songs right now. I'm going through a period of intake. I used to call it writer's block; now I just regard it as a tight ship.

"We're free to make our own timetable for the next LP. We're not ruled by medieval puppet masters, and don't have to make another LP until next year. In terms of competition, there's nothing that comes close to the band. It's all too easy to become bored with it. The game is won. My ambitions are wide, which is why I'm still interested in film—another game with its own kind of chaos."

But rumors were rife that Sting had already begun

working on a solo album, and Andy had predicted when the band might break up in a *Creem* interview the year before. "I think the end will come if someone's career just gets so amazing they don't want to be in the group anymore."

The first reports came in nonetheless through the Associated Press wire that the Police would be disbanding after their March 4, 1984, show in Sydney, Australia.

The response from manager Miles Copeland was immediate. The Police would not be breaking up. "This band is going to be around for a long time," he was quoted by United Press International. Still, nobody can deny that the Police, currently on sabbatical during most of 1984, are taking some well-deserved time off.

Sting was reported to be planning a private expedition in search of the abominable snowman with a veteran yeti hunter. There were rumors he would appear as Pontius Pilate in Martin Scorsese's *Last Temptation of Christ*, a project that never came off, and that he would take the lead role in a BBC version of *Threepenny Opera*. He told several journalists he was considering the part of Ariel in the Royal Shakespeare Company production of *The Tempest* but was more excited at the prospect of playing Caliban, the deformed slave. "There's a character you can get something out of," he said.

Instead, Sting agreed to appear opposite *Flashdance*'s Jennifer Beales as Dr. Frankenstein in *The Bride*, a remake of *The Bride of Frankenstein* directed by Franc Roddam, who was at the helm of Sting's film debut in *Quadrophenia*. The movie is scheduled for release in summer of 1985; Sting filmed his parts throughout Europe during summer of 1984.

In the spring Sting won the prestigious role of Mick in the film version of David Hare's hit Broadway show *Plenty* opposite Meryl Streep and costarring fellow pop star Tracey Ullman. Sting would play a working-class cockney chosen to father the calculating Streep's child, then left by the wayside.

Although he hasn't yet had a box-office success in the movies, Sting's acting career probably represents the biggest danger to the Police's continued existence as a working unit.

"Music has given me the confidence that somewhat prepared me for being in front of a camera," he said. "Making transitions is the hardest thing for a performer to do. I think the performers who have managed to make the transition from one form to another are unusually clever. David Bowie and Bobby Darin both did it quite skillfully."

Even while resting, the Police continued to be in front of the public eye. *Police: Around the World*, the documentary shot on the 1980 world tour by Derek and Kate Burbidge, was released as a home video, followed in the fall of 1984 by *The Police: the Synchronicity Concert*. The band won two Grammy honors, while Sting as a solo performer took a pair himself. The Police earned Best Performance by a Duo or Group for "Every Breath You Take" and Best Rock Performance by a Duo or Group for *Synchronicity*. Sting took home the statue for writing the Song of the Year, "Every Breath," and, ironically, for the third time in the band's history, Best Rock Instrumental Performance for the title track from the *Brimstone and Treacle* LP. By the middle of 1984 *Outlandos D'Amour*, *Zenyatta Mondatta*, *Ghost in the Machine*, and *Synchronicity* had all earned platinum album status, with just *Reggatta de Blanc* still at "only" gold.

As summer 1984 drew to a close, there was another flurry of Police-related activity. A plagiarism claim against Sting reportedly tied up all royalties due him from "Every Breath You Take," alleging he had copied it from an old reggae tune. Andy Summers joined Sting in pursuing a film career by hiring a Hollywood-based agent to seek properties for him to star in and produce. He also collaborated on another album with Robert Fripp, *Bewitched*, which he recorded after the conclusion of the last Police tour.

He told *USA Today* on August 8, 1984, once again, the Police had no intention of breaking up. "People think we are or we're at odds with each other, which is the complete opposite of what's really happening. We're planning to release a live album in spring of 1985 from our performances on the last tour.

"When we go into the studio we're totally committed to the work at hand. There's nothing in the outside world that interferes with our creative process once we're in the studio. Our music has always been visual, so working on films was a natural evolution for us."

The motion picture triple play was completed when it was announced that Stewart Copeland would be following up his critically praised soundtrack for *Rumble Fish* with a score for *Flashdance* director Adrian Lyne's follow-up, the steamy *9½ Weeks*, starring Mickey Rourke and Kim Basinger.

On video fronts, the Police's "Every Breath You Take" received a total of seven nominations in the First Annual MTV Video Music Awards held in September 1984.

Andy Summers commented, "Rock videos tend to leave me very cold after a while. The Police try to go against what everyone else is doing in videos. It's dumb to put a pretty girl in a video for no reason. To me it says that the song isn't enough to stand on its own."

Just before going to press, Summers announced his agent would be accepting film scripts for the guitarist's acting debut while Stewart Copeland appeared in his first feature, *The Rhythmatist*, about African music. And in a long-anticipated move, Sting revealed he would begin recording his debut solo album in Fall 1984 with I.R.S. Records' trio Torch Song—William Orbit, Laurie Mayer, and Grant Gilbert—producing. The album was scheduled for release in early 1985.

By the end of summer 1984, the future appeared to be bright for the Police, as a band and as individuals.

EPILOGUE

*S*o where do they go from here? What will they do next? Will Sting leave the band to pursue Hollywood stardom? Will Andy and Stewart go back to being professional "musos"? Can the Police survive having all their wishes come true?

Very complex questions, of course. First of all Sting is still, to read between his gripes, very much committed to the group. As he confessed, he has a great desire for freedom, but he "needs the group. They're the best musicians I could work with." If it's a musical career he wants...

But Sting is nobody's fool. He realizes the Police are, and always have been, more than the sum of their individual parts brought together by circumstance and fate. And while their every move has been documented by the media, the Police's climb to the top was by no means a calculated, planned assault. With the savvy of Miles Copeland and their own stamina and talent, the Police rode the waves of opportunity and played the game to the hilt, creating much memorable music along the way. It isn't likely that the three of them can duplicate that output separately.

"The reason we stay together is because we still work as a band," Sting said. "As I've said all along, it might break up tomorrow. As soon as it becomes a drag, then that's it: I'll walk out."

It's hard to imagine Sting away from the spotlight for long. "My favorite moments of the set are when we stop playing and singing and I allow the audience to tumble in," he admitted. "I love the way they just get sucked in: WHOOSH!! It confirms you as someone who has given them something, and at the same time, it makes them work, like real art should. An audience has its role, too. They have to work and give something to complete the event."

This remarkably creative group, who have effortlessly fused the experimental and commercial still has more than just music left in it. Not to mention the ubiquitous Miles Copeland prodding them from behind. By spring of 1985 the oft-delayed live album Andy Summers talked about should finally arrive, followed by a disc of new material that truly shows off the band's three-sided nature. The Police are perhaps the only group that could get away with a band LP that features solo sides from each of them... without the others. It is the combination itself, though, all of them together, that provides the winning formula, the mysterious synchronicity that makes the whole thing tick.

"The deeper we go, the less material things become. We see that what we thought were solid atomic particles have qualities and functions that are illogical. I think our salvation is in those little molecules somewhere. The future is not material, it's spiritual," said Sting. "It's like we're looking at the universe through a very powerful microscope and we're going to come out the other end. We're discovering that the universe is not built on and held together by hard little atoms, because these atoms and the spaces between them aren't filled with solid particles; they're filled with *magic*."

APPENDIXES

DISCOGRAPHY

Albums—American Releases

Outlandos D'Amour (A&M, 1978)
Next to You
So Lonely
Roxanne
Hole in My Life
Peanuts
Can't Stand Losing You
Truth Hits Everybody
Born in the 50's
Be My Girl—Sally
Masoko Tango

Reggatta de Blanc (A&M, 1979)
Message in a Bottle
Reggatta de Blanc
It's Alright for You
Bring on the Night
Deathwish
Walking on the Moon
On Any Other Day
The Bed's Too Big without You
Contact
Does Everyone Stare
No Time This Time

Zenyatta Mondatta (A&M, 1980)

Don't Stand So Close to Me
Driven to Tears
When the World Is Running Down, You Make the Best
　　of What's Still Around
Canary in a Coalmine
Voices inside My Head
Bombs Away
De Do Do Do De Da Da Da
Behind My Camel
Man in a Suitcase
Shadows in the Rain
The Other Way of Stopping

Ghost in the Machine (A&M, 1981)

Spirits in the Material World
Every Little Thing She Does Is Magic
Invisible Sun
Hungry for You (j'aurais toujours faim de toi)
Demolition Man
Too Much Information
Rehumanize Yourself
One World (Not Three)
Omegaman
Secret Journey
Darkness

Synchronicity (A&M, 1983)

Synchronicity
Walking in Your Footsteps
O My God
Mother
Miss Gradenko
Synchronicity II
Every Breath You Take

King of Pain
Wrapped Around Your Finger
Tea in the Sahara

Singles

Fall Out/Nothing Achieving (U.K. only)	1977, reissued 1979
Roxanne/Dead End Job (Peanuts in U.K.)	1979
Can't Stand Losing You/No Time This Time (B side Dead End Job in U.K.)	1979
Message in a Bottle/Landlord	1979
Bring on the Night/Visions of the Night	1979
De Do Do do De Da Da Da/ Friends (B side A Sermon in U.K.)	1980
Don't Stand So Close to Me/A Sermon (B side Friends in U.K.)	1980
Every Little Thing She Does Is Magic/Shambelle (B side Flexible Strategies in U.K.)	1981
Spirits in the Material World/ Flexible Strategies (B side Low Life in U.K.)	1982
Every Breath You Take/Murder by Numbers	1983
Wrapped Around Your Finger/ Someone to Talk To	1983
Synchronicity 2/Once Upon a Daydream	1983
King of Pain/Tea in the Sahara	1984

VIDEOGRAPHY

Singles

Can't Stand Losing You (Derek Burbidge)

Roxanne (Derek Burbidge)

So Lonely (Derek Burbidge)

Message in a Bottle (Derek Burbidge)

Walking on the Moon (Derek Burbidge)

Bring on the Night (Derek Burbidge)

Don't Stand So Close to Me (Derek Burbidge)

De Do Do Do De Da Da Da (Derek Burbidge)

Voices Inside My Head (Derek Burbidge)

Every Little Thing She Does Is Magic (Derek Burbidge)

Invisible Sun (Derek Burbidge)

Spirits in the Material World (Derek Burbidge)

Demolition Man (Derek Burbidge)

Every Breath You Take (Kevin Godley and Lol Creme)

Wrapped Around Your Finger (Kevin Godley and Lol Creme)

Synchronicity 2 (Kevin Godley and Lol Creme)

Full Length Videos

Police Around the World (Kate and Derek Burbidge)

The Police: the Synchronicity Concert (Kevin Godley and Lol Creme)

FAN CLUB INFORMATION

Police Fan Club
% Bennett & Associates
8335 Hollywood Boulevard
Los Angeles, CA 90069

ABOUT THE AUTHOR

Ray Nikart is the pen name for a well-known *rockonteur* and pop journalist whose work has appeared in *Musician*, *Music & Sound Output*, *Creem*, *Melody Maker*, *Hit Parader*, and the *Record*.